SIX YÜAN PLAYS

ADVISORY EDITOR: BETTY RADICE

Liu Jung-en was born in Hangchow, China, in 1908 and educated at Yenching University, Peking, and Balliol College, Oxford. Formerly an associate professor in the National Nankai University of China, he has published in Chinese five books of poetry and a novel.

SIX YÜAN PLAYS

Translated with an Introduction by
Liu Jung-en

Penguin Books

PENGUIN BOOKS

Published by the Penguin Group
Penguin Books Ltd, 27 Wrights Lane, London W8 5TZ, England
Penguin Books USA Inc., 375 Hudson Street, New York, New York 10014, USA
Penguin Books Australia Ltd, Ringwood, Victoria, Australia
Penguin Books Canada Ltd, 10 Alcorn Avenue, Toronto, Ontario, Canada M4V 3B2
Penguin Books (NZ) Ltd, 182–190 Wairau Road, Auckland 10, New Zealand

Penguin Books Ltd, Registered Offices: Harmondsworth, Middlesex, England

This translation first published 1972
7 9 10 8 6

Printed in England by Clays Ltd, St Ives plc
Set in Monotype Bembo

CONTENTS

INTRODUCTION

From the end of the Sung dynasty (960–1279) to the end of the Yüan dynasty (1280–1369) a large number of 'music dramas' were written and produced in North China. Out of some 700 known ones about 150 are extant. They are called *tsa chü* ('mixed entertainments'), because in one work the entertainers sang, spoke, played music, danced, mimed and acted. The audience was being entertained on several levels at the same time. The misnamed Peking Opera is their natural descendant. Poetry sung to music occupied a predominant part. These plays are popularly known in China as *Yüan ch'ü* ('Yüan songs'), Yüan Northern Drama. They form an interesting genre of their own and deserve attention. These six Yüan plays are translated for those who are interested in the development of drama in general and of Chinese drama in particular, but who are unfamiliar with Chinese.

The Chinese drama came later than the ancient Greek and the classical Hindu drama, and in the development of Chinese literary forms drama came of age only after poetry and before the novel. While the Chinese populace went to see *The Orphan of Chao* people in England were watching *The Harrowing of Hell.*

The House of Sung was tottering, and in 1127 the Kin people from the North captured the Sung ex-emperor Hui Tsung and his son, the reigning emperor, Ch'in Tsung, and reigned over North China for about one hundred years. Part of the Sung court escaped to the South and proclaimed the seventh son of the ex-emperor Hui Tsung as Emperor Kao Tsung of the new Southern Sung dynasty in Hangchou. The dynasty lasted 152 years. In 1276 the Mongols, a mixed tribe of Tan-tan, Tungus, Turks and Hsiung-nu from the northern parts of Central Asia, having overthrown the Kins took prisoner the last emperor of Sung, Emperor Kung, and two empress dowagers, Hsieh and Ch'üan, and carried them off to the North. The Sung forces retreated to Fukien and then to Yai-shan Island, south of Hsin-hui, Kwangtung. In 1279 General Lu Hsiu-fu, who could not bear to have a young emperor (a younger brother of the last emperor) captured and insulted, took him up on his back and leaped into the sea, and both were drowned. Thus the Sung dynasty came to an end.

Before the Mongols had completed the conquest of China they had already tasted the sweet fruits of many superior cultures in Asia and Europe, and, more or less assimilating them, had become rapidly civilized. By the time Kublai Khan mounted the throne in China in 1280 his court was known throughout the world for its splendour. The names of Jenghiz Khan, Kublai Khan, Marco Polo, Cathay, all recall for us the Yüan dynasty. The Mongol troops were militarily brilliant, sweeping over Europe unchecked as far as modern Czechoslovakia and Venice, where for the first time East met West and traffic between the two began. Politically, outside China, the Mongol empire soon gave rise to numerous rebellions and independent kingdoms of petty khans. Inside China, where the power of the Mongols was to be felt administratively and economically, they adopted existing systems with a dash of savagery. For eighty-nine years they ruled over the Chinese as the Yüan dynasty.

As the Mongols settled down they allotted all the important positions in the government to their fellow horsemen, and gave land to the aristocracy, officials and priests, who turned the farmers into tenants or slaves. Their warlike nomad civilization from the north put the clock back a full era in many parts of China. 'The Han [Chinese] people are of no use to the nation. We can do away with them and turn their land into pasture.' Such was the opinion of the Mongol autocracy. Though it was not carried out throughout China proper, in North China sheep and cattle grazed on hundreds of thousands of acres of very productive agricultural land. The people of the empire they divided into four classes: Mongols; peoples of the minority races in the west; Northern Chinese, Khitan Tartars, Nü-chên Tartars, Koreans; and Southern Chinese. The Southern Chinese had resisted the invaders most vigorously. When a Mongol committed a murder he was exiled, but a Chinese who murdered was executed; when a

Mongol beat a Chinese the Chinese was not allowed to return the blow; the Chinese were not permitted to have weapons of any kind, to hunt, learn military arts, rear horses, pray in a group, or hold fairs. A curfew was imposed every night and lights were forbidden. During the conquest of the Southern Sung dynasty all males of two hundred cities were massacred and women and children enslaved. In the other cities which surrendered all the Chinese were made slaves. Thus slaves acquired in war became so numerous that a slave trade flourished and Chinese slaves were sold overseas. It was recorded that in the seventh year of the period of Ta Tê of Emperor Ch'ang Tsung (1304) at one inquiry 18,473 corrupt officials were condemned, bribes of 45,865 ingots of silver (?) were discovered, and 5,176 sentences passed on prisoners were proved to be unjust. In 1337, when the Yüan dynasty was on the verge of collapse, the emperor was advised to kill all those who bore the surnames of Chang, Wang, Liu, Li and Chao, these being the surnames of the majority of Chinese.

As early as the autumn of the ninth year of Emperor T'ai Tsung (1238), while the occupation of China still continued, the last imperial examination for the civil service was held, and it was not held again until the August of 1314. Anyone who had ever studied a book in the days of imperial China had had as his ultimate aim to sit for the imperial examination – the only chance in his life by which he could raise himself up in the world as a scholar-official. Now this very road to personal success was blocked. Many fell away, and others turned to other pursuits. A few turned to literary endeavours of a popular form, especially the drama.

As the imperial examination was abolished, so was Confucianism and all it stood for. The mode of life and thought that governed the scholars – eventually the officials and the perpetuators of an entire system of Chinese life – felt its foundations suddenly give way. Confucianism became worse than nothing. The Mongols degraded the Confucian scholars to the ninth class of subjects, lower than the prostitutes who came into the eighth class and only one class higher than the bottom-most, the beggars. Some were dismayed, some in despair; some no doubt rejoiced. Now much of the Confucian conservatism that had stood in the way of the true creative power of the Chinese genius was being swept away. For the first time for many a long year the intellectuals could breathe fresh air. As the new masters of China did not care much for ideas, so ideas flourished among the Chinese. Conformity, respect and loyalty to the wrong persons for the wrong reasons, the near religious worship of Confucius as a national sage and saviour – all these were gone, while Taoism, Buddhism, Mohammedanism, Christianity and other faiths which had hitherto been looked at askance by official Confucianism now began freely to gain ground. A new intellectual freedom was born and found its expression in the drama. And the Mongols, in spite of their distaste for intellectual pursuits, loved and encouraged it as an excellent form of entertainment. Musicians and singers accompanied their troops wherever they went.

After years of war the master race settled down to enjoy the amenities of civilized Chinese life, oblivious to the well-concealed attacks upon their inhumanity and to the fun poked at their extravagant gestures of power and justice. The drama was to be the weapon of the conquered. The response was immediate and the result instantaneous. The creative impulse was at last released from the shackles of orthodox literary standards. What was to be expressed had seldom been expressed before in poetry, prose or any other form. Once again the hope and aspiration of the Chinese people had found an outlet. But alas, the theatre was not to enjoy its new-found freedom long. When another Chinese empire, the Ming dynasty – wiser but more cold-blooded – came once more to rule its own people, censorship was rigorously enforced. Anyone who put on, had printed, or was found in possession of plays of a certain kind was to be executed together with all the members of his family.

It was not until the thirteenth century that the Chinese drama as we understand the term emerged, and it grew out of poetry. It was not only late in coming, but was never taken seriously or regarded as orthodox literature worthy of the endeavour of Confucian scholars or the attention of the educated reader. Actors and actresses were placed in the same class as prostitutes, barbers and corn-removers, and like them their sons were forbidden to take part in the imperial examination.

Chinese poetry had found its full expression in the T'ang dynasty (618–907) some six centuries before, and had passed through many stages of development. As social conditions changed Chinese poetical form evolved accordingly, to suit the tastes of succeeding generations. By the time of the Sung dynasty the prevailing form was *tz'ŭ*.* In the Yüan dynasty it gave way to *san ch'ü*, which was of two kinds: *hsiao ling* and *t'ao shu*. Being recitative in nature, *t'ao shu* in the hands of the Yüan dramatists came into its own. That the new social condition and *t'ao shu* should come together to give birth to Yüan drama will always be hailed as a most happy literary event.

Systematic studies of Chinese drama began only with Wang Kuo-wei (1877–1927), one of the great scholars of the turn of the century. His *History of Sung and Yüan Drama* published in 1915 was the first book of its kind, by which time the activities of the Yüan dramatists had been over for six hundred years. The Chinese being great theatre-goers there has been no lack of records of the drama and the theatre; people have written anecdotes, memoirs and personal comments, and have collected quotations relating to actors, actresses, impresarios, singers, musicians, theatres, audiences and their activities as part of the social history of their towns and times, but generally this has only been to add to the confusion of our knowledge of the Chinese theatre.

From a hundred years of feverish dramatic activity there are about a hundred Yüan dramatists whose names have come down to us, and the titles of some six or seven hundred plays. There must have been more than that number, however, if we remember the vogue of vandalism, private and official, in Chinese history. *Lu Kuei Pu* (*A Record of Living and Dead Ghosts* – 1330),† written by Chung Szŭ-

*Definitions of Chinese literary terms in a few words in English will not be adequate here. Studious readers are referred to the many scholarly articles and books in English where such terms are explained.

†Revised twice: once between 1333 and 1341 and again, with additional material, by Chai Chung-ming (1343–1422).

ch'êng (1279?–1360?), a dramatist himself, divided Yüan dramatists into three stages according to the grandfather, father and contemporary generations. The first stage covered about fifty years when the Mongols vanquished the Kins, occupied North China, overthrew the Sung and completed their conquest of China. Most of the dramatists belonged to this stage, a long period of activity and also the most memorable, during which most of the masterpieces were produced. The centre of their activities was the capital Ta-tu, the modern Peking, and they were all Northern Chinese except one, a Nü-chên Tartar, Li Chih-fu. Chung Szŭ-ch'êng also divided the dramatists into two groups: those who belonged to the official ruling class and those who were professional playwrights belonging to playwrights' guilds. It was the latter who were responsible for bringing Yüan drama to the position it occupies in Chinese literature; when new plays were needed the theatrical companies would have to approach the gentlemen of the guilds, and it was generally found to be no easy matter.

Nearly all Yüan dramatists turned for their material to old stories from the country's long history, to popular legends, narrative poems, or early simple plays. Each time an historical episode or character or an old story was used, new blood was transfused into the well-loved tales. They were used to speak to their contemporaries of the problems facing them, and to remind the native Chinese of their terrible plight under a foreign yoke. The playwrights saw to it that the Mongol rulers and their henchmen who oppressed them were ridiculed and their administration satirized. The faithful and the virtuous were rewarded, the wicked and the treacherous brought to book, the meek and lowly extolled, and the powerful and mighty brought low. Lovers were separated and reunited or torn apart for ever. Finding their immediate life hard and distressing it was no wonder that playwrights also turned their minds to the worlds of sexual love, of fantasy and supernatural beings. New ideas born of desperation were freely presented and discussed. The dramatists sang of the sorrows of a conquered people, and, what was more important, of justice, humanity and freedom, even if that freedom was only of the mind. Formerly most intellectuals had written to please the orthodox authorities; now there were none to please but themselves. Chu Ch'üan, Prince Hsien of Ning in the late fourteenth century, scholar, dramatist, the sixteenth son of the founder of the Ming dynasty, divided Yüan plays into twelve categories according to their subject in his book on music, drama and song *T'ai Ho Chêng Yin P'u* (*True Harmony* – 1398): the subjects were 1. human beings who become gods and immortals, 2. hermits, 3. emperors and officials, 4. loyal officials and martyrs, 5. the filial, the faithful, the incorruptible, the chaste, 6. the treacherous and the slanderous censured and rebuked, 7. orphans and exiles, 8. knights errant and warriors in action, 9. lovers, 10. sorrows of parting, joys of meeting, 11. courtesans, 12. Buddhist and other gods.

In form some have seen the influence of the ancient Hindu classical drama on Yüan plays, by way of *hsi wên* ('dramatic writings') of the Sung dynasty. A very old Sanskrit manuscript of a section of Kalidasa's *Shakuntala* was discovered in the twenties (?) in Kuo Ch'ing Temple in Mount T'ien T'ai, Chekiang; Mount T'ien T'ai is near Wên-chou, the home of *hsi wên*. What exactly *hsi wên* was we do not know, as only fragments of it have survived, though being in the nature of a spoken narrative it could well have been an important stage in the development of Chinese drama before the arrival of Yüan plays.

Yüan plays are usually of four acts each, with very few exceptions. Some have a *hsieh tzŭ* ('wedge')* at the beginning or in between acts. This is neither a prologue nor an interlude, but an integral part of the play. It has a unity of its own though it is not independent, the dramatic idea contained in it being insufficient to make it an act. It is to steady the construction of the play as a wedge does any structure.

A Yüan play was primarily written to be sung and acted. The poetic form of the sung passages – the arias or lyrics – used in Yüan plays was *t'ao shu* of *san ch'ü*, as we have already mentioned, with

*Not to be confused with the 'wedge' in Bach's Prelude and Fugue in E Minor, 'The Wedge', B.W.V 548; no relation, except as an element of synthesis.

some modifications for greater freedom and naturalness. Each act of a Yüan play contained one song sequence of about ten lyrics of different length, each lyric limited to one repeated rhyming sound. Each song sequence had a distinctive and definite metre and a definite tone pattern. Each sequence of lyrics had a unified mood of feeling, and each lyric was written to a pre-existing tune, some of which were very ancient. Out of 28 sequences of 335 tunes the Yüan dramatists used about 9. With a few exceptions the leading man or woman sang throughout the play, and the participation of other players was confined to spoken dialogue. Between the lyrics occurred the dialogue which carried forward the story. The lyrics also conveyed this but to a lesser degree, more often than not repeating what the dialogue had already stated. Presumably the dialogue existed for the sake of the lyrics; however, some believe that the dialogue of a Yüan play was at least as interesting and accomplished as the lyrics, if not more so. The language used in it was the vernacular of the day, and the Yüan dramatists had raised it to artistic perfection. Here was the living, vigorous language of everyday usage employed to express ideas and feelings truly and sincerely, without any literary embellishments, and placed side by side in competition with the near classical language of the lyrics. The dialogue was long and full, and if we omit the lyrics from the plays they still remain splendid plays. We have editions of Yüan plays with all the lyrics only, and one reads them as poetry.

Wang Shih-chên (1526–91) of the Ming dynasty in his *I Yüan Chih Yen* (*Thoughts on the Arts*) had this to say about the tunes and poetry of Yüan drama: The tunes of Yüan plays were all from the North and like its people were powerful and grave, heroic and elegant, noble and simple, liable to be a little rough; their strength rested on the stringed instruments, principally on *p'i pa*; more words were used and at the same time the tunes had *ts'u* (something between agitato and animato), and where there was *ts'u* one felt their vigour; they accorded well with the lyrics; the feeling of the words was more pronounced and the feeling of the music less.

The musical instruments used to accompany the lyrics were probably these:* the *san hsien*, a three-stringed plucked instrument; the *p'i pa*, a four-stringed (at that time – more strings were added later) plucked instrument; the *shêng*, consisting of thirteen pipes of different lengths forming a circle each with a finger hole and having a mouth-piece through which the musician blows and sucks; the *ti*, flute; *lo*, gong; *ku*, drum; *pan*, wooden clappers. The *san hsien* or *p'i pa* were the more important instruments. Though all these instruments have with slight modifications remained in use to the present, the music performed in Yüan drama is a matter on which I must refer the reader to experts in Chinese music.

We still have treatises on the art of singing, often written in such fanciful, rhetorical and abstract terms that it is difficult to form any idea of what they really meant. In *T'ai Ho Chêng Yin P'u* there were listed the names of thirty-six famous Yüan singers, four of whom received a few lines to describe their art. One such was Li Liang-ch'ên whose voice was described as *chüeh* (*chüeh* being the third note, 'mi', of the ancient Chinese pentatonic scale). *Chüeh* was the property of the element wood; its quality was straightforwardness; in terms of an empire it represented the people; it was of the colour green; in the heavens it corresponded to the planet Wood (Jupiter); in terms of human virtues, it was loving-kindness; in terms of the seasons, it was spring. Doubtless it would take a Yüan Chinese to appreciate Mr Li's art. The description went on to say that his voice was like a green dragon (not the kind of dragon that St George slew) singing beside autumn waters. Once, amid the commotion of an army and ten thousand cavalry soldiers, Mr Li started to sing, and not a single brave warrior failed to stop and prick up his ears. Singers were warned against some of the worst habits to be avoided. While singing one must not unnecessarily open or shut one's lips, shake one's head, snap one's fingers or stamp one's feet. One's highest aim should be to have one's singing likened to a wandering cloud flying in the sky with nothing standing in its way above or below. This would be the true harmony of heaven and earth. And for this the Yüan singers enjoyed quite a lucrative profession.

*Illustrated on p. 281.

The devices of aside, soliloquy and unashamed address to the audience were a matter of course. Coincidences were the rule not the exception. When A expects B, B and no one else is sure to appear. When each character except the very minor ones appeared, he or she invariably introduced himself to the audience; and as though once was not enough, it was repeated at every subsequent appearance so there could be no mistaking his identity. Sometimes he recited a doggerel which could be in praise of his or her profession, in summary of a philosophy of life, or in downright self-ridicule. Many lines were common property and used by different dramatists in the mouths of different characters. Naïvety and sophistication proved most congenial bedfellows in Yüan drama. At the end of a performance usually the last character who sang or spoke came forward to read the title and theme of the play. The world here was indeed a stage.

No attempt was made to have things realistic; far from it. It was the imaginative experience that the audience was sharing with the dramatist. Location was indicated by the performer or through conversation. Time and distance were almost non-existent. Night followed day in the twinkling of an eye. The map was calculated any mile to the inch.

This kind of play is not altogether unfamiliar to western readers of drama. The audience had to supply the décor, and was constantly reminded of the fact that life as represented on the stage was now art and theatre.

CELESTINA: . . . Go into the closet where I keep the ointments, and you'll find it in that black cat's skin, where I told you to put the she-wolf's eyes. Bring down the goat's blood too, and those bits of his whiskers that you cut off.

ELICIA: Here they all are, Mother. Take them.*

Here Elicia, in full view of the audience and without moving a step, had 'gone and returned' with the things Celestina wanted.

*Fernando de Rojas, *The Spanish Bawd*, tr. J. M. Cohen, Penguin Books, 1964, p. 68.

HELEN: This is Egypt; here flows the virgin river, the lovely Nile. . . . My name is Helen. Now let me tell you of my misfortunes.*

Stage directions in brackets indicated what class of player was to play a particular role – the leading man, the supporting man, the clown or someone else, telling him what expression he should use, what he was to do, what he was to wear, what he was to carry and whether he was to speak or sing what was to follow. Some editions have the stage directions in detail at the beginning of the play, some at the end. Stage properties were plainly mentioned in them, whether collars, scarves, coats, skirts, stockings, shoes, beards, handkerchiefs, beads, fans, etc. In one Yüan play one reads 'Enter the leading man riding on a bamboo horse.' A stick with a horse's head between the actor's legs is unthinkable. Probably it was something like the hobby-horse in a morris dance: the figure of a horse in bamboo-work in two parts fastened to the performer. Sound effects included 'A cock crows,' 'A wild goose cries,' 'Thunder rolls,' among others.

The stage was presumably bare except for a couple of chairs and a table. There were one or two (probably two) doors for the entrance and exit of the actors, called *kuei mên tao* ('the gates of the ghosts') because the personages the performers impersonated had all passed away. They *were* ghosts after all. The 'doors', however, might not actually have been doors but simply passages. The only representation of the staging of these plays that still exists is a Yüan fresco in Kuang Shêng Temple in Mount Huo, Chao-ch'êng, Shansi, depicting a scene from a play about immortals, on a stage with a backcloth of two huge landscape paintings: one with a figure, the other with a dragon, placed side by side.

We presume that the acting was highly stylized. Actors generally played female roles, and actresses sometimes male roles. Each actor or actress was trained to play a particular type – the leading man, the leading lady, the clown – although in a small troupe one player would be expected to play anybody and any part. The characters were of

*Euripides, *The Bacchae and Other Plays*, tr. Philip Vellacott, Penguin Books, 1954, pp. 125–6.

four types: 1. *mo*, male parts, 2. *tan*, female parts, 3. *ching*, 'character' parts, 4. *tsa tung*, supernumeraries. There was also another form of classification, not by names of parts but by roles: for example, according to age, *p'ei lao* (old peasant), *pu erh* (old woman or procuress); according to profession, *ku* (official), *hsi suan* (scholar), *pan ko* (village bully), *i tz'ŭ* (soldier), *pang lao* (murderer), etc. Each *ching* had a dab of white on his or her nose. Certain characters had a dark complexion, and stage directions usually indicated that some dark pigment was to be used. Apart from this, however, it seems that little paint was used on the face.

Many large cities in Yüan times had theatrical districts, and each district had a score of theatres. Some large ones could accommodate thousands of spectators. Apart from the permanent theatres there were temporary ones built of wooden scaffolding – it is recorded in a contemporary source that one of this type collapsed and about forty people were killed. A theatre built in the Yüan dynasty was discovered in 1932 in the city of Ten Thousand Springs in the province of Shansi. An anonymous Yüan play entitled *Han Chung-li Made the Actor Lan Ts'ai-ho an Immortal* and a *t'ao ch'ü* by Tu Shan-fu of Yüan entitled *A Country Cousin Has No Idea of a Theatre* give us a pretty good idea of what a Yüan theatre looked like. Our Cousin, passing through one of the thoroughfares, saw colourful posters announcing the names of the plays and performers. He made his way to where large crowds of people were surging and clamouring, coming at last to a piece of fenced-in ground. At the door a man was shouting at the top of his voice: 'Come in! come in! No seats for latecomers! First-class acting! Showing today – ' and he would proceed to announce the names of certain acts and performers. Our Cousin was allowed in on paying 200 cashes (20 coppers) as an admission fee. First he walked up a wooden ramp and saw around him tier upon tier of people sitting. Above him he saw something like a bell tower, and below him people milling around like a whirlpool. When he found himself in the pit he saw on both sides 'stalls' where people sat row upon row, and facing the bell tower a stage protruding on three sides into the pit. At the side of the stage, where the musicians were, he saw actresses or prostitutes or actress-prostitutes sitting, looking like rows of beast-head tiles on a rooftop. Each of them had her light blue skirt tightly drawn around her buttocks and her black silk scarf closely wrapped round her head, and on all sides they made eyes at the blades of the day in the audience.

Performances were given mainly by two groups: one composed of professionals and amateurs, and the other of prostitutes, both male and female. In *Ch'ing Lou Chih* (*Records of the Green Pavilion*) Hsia T'ing-chih (1316?–66?) wrote the lives of, among others, seventy courtesans, and nearly all of them were singers, musicians, dancers or actresses. Brothels also staged performances of plays. Apparently the inmates carried on two professions at the same time. Many actors appeared under the names of their wives, advertising themselves for example as 'Yen Shan-hsiu's husband Ma Erh'. Obviously the wife enjoyed a greater reputation.

Northern Yüan plays are not performed today.

For the last three hundred years the most popular collection of Yüan plays has been *Yüan Ch'ü Hsüan* (*Selected Yüan Plays*), compiled and edited by Tsang Tsin-shu of Ch'ang-hsing in the forty-fourth year of Wan Li (1616) in the Ming dynasty. Another collection, the three-volume *Yüan Ch'ü Hsüan Wai Pien* (*Supplements to Selected Yüan Plays*) edited by Sui Shu-shên, was brought out in 1959 by the Chung Hua Book Company in Peking. This and *Selected Yüan Plays* comprise nearly all the Yüan plays now extant. Both collections contain plays by early Ming dramatists. Fragments of Yüan plays have been collected by Chao Ching-shên in his *Yüan Jên Tsa Chü Kuo Ch'en* (*Fragments of Plays by Yüan Dramatists*) published by Ku Tien Wên Hsüeh Ch'u Pan Shê (Classic Literature Press, Shanghai, 1956).

The editor of *Selected Yüan Plays*, as he wrote in his preface, had in his private collection many rare Yüan plays besides the well-known ones, and he had borrowed from a certain Liu Yen-pai two hundred manuscripts copied from some editions in the palace. The hundred plays in his selection were very carefully and sometimes drastically edited (as was found when older editions were discovered and scholars compared them); dialogue and stage directions were completed, words corrected, and the pronunciation of certain words indicated. Later critics have condemned him for tampering with the texts of some of the plays in his collection, and suspected him of consigning many masterpieces to oblivion. However, we must be grateful to him at least for preserving many plays for us in a readable form. The editor of *Supplements to Selected Yüan Plays* had many advantages over Tsang Tsin-shu in having available much recent research done in the field of Yüan drama and several newly discovered collections of Yüan plays. As a result he has given us a very useful and necessary collection, a great contribution to the study of Yüan drama, expertly edited. The plays are printed in chronological order.

For my six plays I have used the edition *Szŭ Pu Pei Yao* which was based on a Ming edition, published in Shanghai by the Chung Hua Book Company under the general editorship of Lu Fei-k'uei, and I have also consulted other editions. The selection of these six plays is purely a matter of personal taste. In each play I have omitted passages in dialogue and in verse which are obscure to me, inessential to the play as a whole, or tiresomely repetitive. No attempt has been made to translate the lyrics into any of the English poetic forms. The lyrics are printed line by line while the dialogue is continuous. Each character is as far as possible given only one name throughout the play, in spite of the multiplicity of personal names in the Chinese. Official titles changed their meaning as dynasties changed. In most cases approximate titles have been used and quite arbitrarily. All footnotes are those of the translator, and in quite a few instances they have been incorporated in the text. If these plays in translation should drive the reader further away from Chinese drama the fault is entirely mine.

Here I should like to record my appreciation of the interest many people have taken in these translations, especially Miss Paddy H. Harding, and my gratitude above all to Howard Davies, to whom I am deeply indebted for many emendations in point of sense and style.

THE ORPHAN OF CHAO

This is a play of vengeance. It takes twenty years and toll of three lives in the process. Vengeance is almost a religious cult in China, zealously pursued from the dawn of its history. The saying 'My enemy shall not share the same heaven with me,' puts the seal of nation-wide approval on the avenger. The gruesomeness of the punishment meted out to Tu-an was only matched by the enormity of his crime. When passion held sway and little justice was done, when a dog could be credited with sagacity and an emperor could be so simple as to believe it, one shouldn't wonder too much at the consequences. To kill the nine generations of your enemy's family (great-great-grandfather, great-grandfather, grandfather, father, enemy himself, son, grandson, great-grandson, great-great-grandson) had been the standard recipe of Chinese emperors and tyrants for exterminating their foes. It was done from fear of vengeance. The greater the occasion for it, the more cruel the method of prevention. To a western reader the play may appear unnatural and bloodthirsty, as indeed it is; but it also shows plainly how instantly, calmly and gladly debts of integrity, gratitude and friendship were paid in order that the ultimate vengeance might be exacted. General Han commits suicide because he is a man of integrity; Ch'êng's son has to die because of the kindness Ch'êng has received; Kung-sun gives up his life because of his friendship for Chao Tun. They die willingly; as we Chinese say, they 'see death as a journey home'.

The sources of this play are mainly *Tso Ch'uan* (*Chronicles of Tso*) by Tso Ch'iu-ming or Tso-ch'iu Ming of the Chou dynasty (1111–256 B.C.) and *Shih Chi* (*Historical Records*) by Ssu-ma Ch'ien (145–*c.*86 B.C.). In the last decade of the seventh century B.C. there lived a certain king, King Ling of Tsin, whose sport it was to shoot at his people with a crossbow from a high tower inside his palace and watch them scatter in panic. Once his cook had served his bear's paw underdone so he had had him beheaded. Chao Tun, a high official, remonstrated with him on both accounts. The king, though he admitted his misdeeds, never changed his way of life and grew moreover to hate Chao Tun. He sent an assassin to kill him but the attempt failed. One day in the ninth month he invited Chao Tun to drink with him, intending to kill him then, but when Hsi Mi-ming, one of Chao's private guards, heard of this he went up and dragged his master away while they were drinking, saying that to drink three cups of wine before one's king and not then to take one's leave would be a disgraceful failure of good manners. Finding his plot fouled the king set his dog upon Chao Tun. Hsi killed the dog before it could savage his master. Immediately the king's bodyguard fell upon them. With Hsi fending off the soldiers and shielding Chao Tun the two men tried to make good their escape, but Hsi was killed in the struggle. At this critical moment a soldier of the king's bodyguard mutinied, attacked his own men, and helped Chao Tun to escape. When asked why he had done this the man replied: 'I was the starving man under the mulberry tree.' Once while out hunting Chao Tun had given this poor man food and wine, but the man had disappeared before he could ask him his name. When the news that Chao Tun was trapped in the palace reached the Chao family, they fought their way in with their private army and with the help of those people who hated the king. King Ling was killed in the midst of his bodyguard together with several of his followers. It was the twenty-seventh of the ninth month. Before Chao Tun reached the frontier to seek asylum in a neighbouring state, peace was restored. King Ch'êng came to the throne and Chao Shuo, Chao Tun's son, married one of the king's elder sisters. In time Chao Tun died. During the reign of King Ching, one of the late king's faithful followers, Tu-an Ku, proclaimed that though Chao Tun had not killed King Ling himself, the idea had been his. Although Chao Tun was dead, his descendants still enjoyed positions in the kingdom and it was plain that the treason had been abetted. A number of high officials agreed with him. General Han defended the Chao family in public, and in private advised Chao Shuo to flee the country; but the latter refused and begged the general to look after his descendants if anything should happen to him. General Han promised. Soon afterwards Tu-an forged a royal decree ordering the slaughter of the entire Chao family. Chao Shuo's wife, the reigning king's aunt, escaped and hid herself in the palace. As the princess was now with child two retainers of Chao Shuo, Kung-sun Ch'u-chiu and Ch'êng Ying, decided together that if it was a son that was born they would save it at all costs, if a daughter they would follow their master and take their own lives. It was a son. Tu-an searched the palace for the child, but the mother put her baby son inside her trousers and prayed: 'If it is the fate of the Chao family to be wiped out, then cry! If it is not, be still.' The child kept silent and Tu-an left empty-handed; but his suspicions remained. 'Which is more difficult: to help the orphan grow up, or repay one's master's kindness by taking one's life and following him?' asked Kung-sun. 'It is more difficult to help the orphan grow up,' replied Ch'êng. 'Then let me do the lesser thing,' Kung-sun answered.

They bought an unwanted child, put on it embroidered clothes, wrapped it up in a piece of brocade and took it to live with them on the other side of Mount Shou Yang. In accordance with their plan Ch'êng went to Tu-an saying, 'I cannot keep the orphan of Chao any longer. If you give me a thousand pieces of gold I'll tell you where you may find him.' Tu-an readily agreed to the payment. When Ch'êng came with Tu-an and his men to the mountain, Kung-sun openly rebuked him for betraying his master and his friend, and cried to Tu-an: 'Kill me but spare the innocent child!' Not only did they kill the 'orphan' but Kung-sun too. For fifteen years Ch'êng was left in safety in the mountain with the real orphan.

More than ten years after the event, General Han found occasion to reveal to the king what in fact had happened to the Chao family without His Majesty's knowledge. The king was touched and distressed, and did not know what to do as not a single descendant of Chao was left. General Han told him the truth. The orphan was secretly brought to the palace with Ch'êng. One day the king was taken ill and officials came to inquire after his health. The king revealed to them the tragedy that had befallen the Chaos, and both Ch'êng and the orphan were presented to them. Now convinced that Tu-an had cheated them, they declared themselves ready to do whatever His Majesty commanded. Tu-an was thereupon executed together with the rest of his family. To the orphan Chao Wu the king restored everything that had belonged to his ancestors. When the youth came of age Ch'êng said to him, 'When you were born there were many willing to die for your family. I remained alive, not because I was unwilling to sacrifice my life, but in order to bring up the only descendant of the family. Now you have come of age, and your hereditary positions and many other honours have been restored to you. It is time for me to die, so that I may report to your grandfather and my old friend Kung-sun. It was Kung-sun who was confident that I was able to perform this task, and he who sacrificed his life first so that I could succeed. If I do not descend to the underworld to tell him, he will think I have failed in my duty.' And with that Ch'êng killed himself.

The stories of the Chao family and its friends have been popular among the Chinese in many literary forms. Yüan dramatists understandably drew from history characters and stories which contained parallels with their times, as have the dramatists of occupied territories at other times in other countries. In this way their lives were not endangered, as they might have been had they by direct comment urged their fellow-countrymen to patriotism and resistance against their oppressors. It has been suggested that the Chao family symbolized the House of Sung (its surname was also Chao) conquered by the Mongols, and that the vengeance was the vengeance of the Chinese people upon the Yüan tyrants.

The method by which Tu-an Ku trained his dog is strangely reminiscent of the plan Dudon, the French knight, used to kill a dragon ravaging the island of Rhodes many centuries ago, as retold by Dr Johnson in one of his *Idler* essays; and the round-up of the children within the Kingdom of Tsin may remind us of the Massacre of the Innocents in Bethlehem.

This play has been translated into many western languages. It caught Voltaire's imagination, and he honoured it by adapting it under the title of *L'Orphelin de la Chine*.

Chi Chün-hsiang wrote eight plays (some say six, some say five), but apart from a fragment of his play *Ch'ên Wên-t'u Attains His Illumination in a Dream under the Shade of a Pine-tree*, this one only is extant. He was a native of Ta-tu. As is the case with most Yüan dramatists we know practically nothing about him.

THE SOUL OF CH'IEN-NÜ LEAVES HER BODY

To the author of this play, Chêng Teh-hui (alias Chêng Kuang-tsu), some eighteen or twenty plays have been credited, but only eight are still in existence, the authenticity of three of which has been questioned. He was a native of Hsiang-ling of P'ing-yau, and had been a government censor in Hang-chou. Traditionally known to be straightforward in all his dealings, he did not suffer fools gladly. He was greatly respected by actors and actresses who addressed him as Venerable Mr Chêng. When he died he was cremated in Ling Chih Temple in the West Lake, Hang-chou. With Kuan Han-ch'ing, Ma Chih-yüan and Pai Jen-fu (alias Pai P'o), he completes the quartet of the foremost Yüan dramatists.

It has been generally agreed that the main source for this play is *Li Hun Chi* (*The Story of a Soul Leaving Its Body*)* by Ch'ên Hsüan-yu of the T'ang dynasty. It runs as follows:

In the third year of the T'ien Shou period (A.D. 692) a certain Chang I of the city of Ch'ing-ho, a hereditary official, made his home in Hêng-chou. He was of quiet disposition and had few friends. He had no son but two daughters, the elder of whom died young. And the virtue and beauty of the younger daughter Ch'ien-niang were without peer. Chang I had a nephew in T'ai-yüan named Wang Chou, who when young was already considered very gifted and whose handsome appearance was the envy of many. Chang I thought much of him, and often mentioned that some day he would make Ch'ien-niang his wife. As they grew up Chou and Ch'ien-niang began night and day to think of each other, though their families knew nothing of this. In time Chou was selected by matchmakers to

*In *Chiu Hsiao Shuo* (*Ancient Tales*), ed. Wu Tsêng-ch'i, Shanghai, 1957.

be married to someone else, and to this Chang I consented. When the news reached Ch'ien-niang she was overcome with distress, and Chou, in great hatred, turned against her father. He succeeded in having himself transferred to the capital, and though entreated not to go, remained resolute.

So they sent him on his way with money and gifts and, bidding them a sad farewell, Chou boarded his boat. At sunset they moored below the hills a few miles beyond the outer wall of the city. It was just after midnight and Chou could not sleep, when suddenly he heard someone on the river-bank walking in great haste. Soon the person had reached the boat. He asked who it was, and found to his amazement that it was Ch'ien-niang walking barefoot who had arrived. Chou nearly went out of his mind with joy. Taking hold of her hands he asked why she had come. In tears she replied: 'What love you have for me! Gradually I was beginning to respond, and now someone has come to deprive me of my hope. But I know how deep and unchanging your love is. I will repay you even to the point of death, and risk a wanderer's life to be with you.' Chou was overjoyed. Immediately he hid Ch'ien-niang in the boat, then taking advantage of the night, they fled. Travelling doubly fast they came at last to Szechuan. There they lived for five years, and two sons were born to them, but all the time they did not write to Chang I. Ch'ien-niang often thought of her parents, however, and one day she came to her husband weeping and said: 'Years ago I could not bear to be unfaithful to you, and I abandoned all my duty to my parents to be with you. But now five years have passed. If I am to stay here still longer I don't know how I'll endure it!' Chou took pity on her and said: 'We shall soon return, rest assured.' And soon afterwards they all went back to Hêng-chou, as he had said.

On arriving Chou went first alone to Chang I's house, and began by begging to be allowed to state his case. 'Ch'ien-niang is ill in her room. Why are you lying to me like this?' asked Chang I. 'But Ch'ien-niang is in the boat,' replied Chou. Chang I was greatly taken aback and sent someone to see if it was true. The man indeed saw Ch'ien-niang in the boat in perfect health. She asked of the messenger whether his master was well. The man was amazed, and running at a great speed returned and reported to Chang I. When the girl in her room heard it, she smiled, rose, changed her clothes, and painted and adorned herself. Smiling still, and saying not a word, she came out and welcomed the other Ch'ien-niang, whereupon the two merged into one perfect form, even their clothing being the same. The families found this uncanny, and would breathe no word of it afterwards except among themselves. Forty years later the husband and wife died leaving three sons, who all became first-class graduates and were promoted to high positions in the kingdom.

This must have been a much celebrated story at the time. Another play (now lost) of the same period by Chao Kung-fu was based on the same material. It is a lovers' ordeal very conveniently solved by soul separating from body and following the beloved. The popular Chinese belief has been that the soul has an independent life of its own. When it leaves the body, the body becomes inanimate and gradually decays if the soul does not return in time. When we say '*hun pu fu t'i*' we mean 'the soul is not with the body', someone has fainted, is in a swoon or has lost consciousness in fear.

Love between man and woman as a subject for art or literature, so widely accepted as it is in the west, was once a subject shunned by strait-laced Confucian China. It was only for libertines and the vulgar herd to mention. The old saying 'In bed husband and wife, out of bed lady and gentleman,' shows plainly that love was something to be done and not to be sung. No respectable parent or elder would allow any young person to read *Chin P'ing Mei*, a novel of the Ch'ing dynasty (1644–1911), or the Yüan play *Hsi Hsiang Chi* (*The Romance of the Western Chamber*). In short, love between man and woman was something to be ashamed of until the modern 'barbarians' from the west taught the Chinese in the present century to raise it to a higher place in human life. Of course there is no lack of love songs, and love stories, or of lovers who have been as gloriously incorrigible as their counterparts in the west.

THE INJUSTICE DONE TO TOU NGO

Injustice seems to have been an obsession with Yüan dramatists, for the obvious reason that justice itself was hard to obtain. And since justice was only hard won from human beings, gods, ghosts and whatnot had to be enlisted to see it was done in this world of mortals. Quite a few temples in China are filled with idols of fearful-looking judges and wardens of hell to warn the living to lead a good life while here on earth so as not to suffer the tortures of the damned in hell when dead. Here superstition is called upon to help justice. Tou Ngo appeals to Heaven and Earth, the customary deities of Truth and Justice, who have been worshipped in China throughout the centuries of its existence. Whenever and wherever a Chinese is in trouble he calls upon Heaven. True, Tou Ngo appeals to her judge, but knowing full well that if justice ever comes it will not come from that quarter. She does it perfunctorily. Though she calls upon Heaven and Earth, she questions their validity and even rebukes them. She knows that they too will only vindicate her innocence with snow in summer and a lingering drought when she is dead and when justice is of no use to her. Yet she submits herself to her execution and is willing to await the ultimate justice. She has to believe in an after-life, and fortunately does – poor impossible ghost in this most possible world. But Nature has been most obliging to poor unfortunate souls in China by suspending its laws now and then, here and there, when they are dead, for the sake of moralizing maxim-mongers and story-tellers to give cold comfort to the hopeless and helpless.

Yüan dramatists had adapted many stories of retribution for the stage. A half-legendary judge was shown in a series of difficult cases which he conducted with the utmost dexterity and justice to all concerned. As there was so little justice in their workaday world, justice in the imaginary world was highly satisfactory. If they could not bring the magistrate in their own city to account, they could at least have his counterpart ridiculed and punished to their hearts' content on the stage. The magistrate here is called Prefect Evilbrute. When he announces 'My coffers are filled from the cases I hear,' this raises knowing smiles from many a face. And when he kneels and says 'Anyone who brings a case before me is father and mother to me; it is he who clothes and feeds me,' many a head may be seen nodding among the audience. The court procedure in the play is too ridiculous to be true, though miscarriages of justice are still possible in a highly organized and civilized society. Injustice was as summary as was justice. The Chinese in the Yüan dynasty had a double burden of injustice to bear: a foreign yoke and a corrupt judicial system.

Tou Ngo is a properly educated child of the old school. Widowhood she prizes, so she accuses her mother-in-law of infidelity and goes into great detail to taunt her. (Some critics are of the opinion that her rebukes are in fact administered to those Chinese who became willing slaves to their new Mongol masters, that it was their disloyalty and infidelity the dramatist was attacking here.) Tou Ngo confesses to the crime because she cannot bear to see her elderly mother-in-law tortured. Then she revolts against Heaven and Earth, the supposed defenders of the innocent. This is significant. It shakes the foundations of age-old religious beliefs deep-rooted in the Chinese character when she accuses them of being accomplices of evil and injustice. Having exhausted all the help a human being can appeal to, she resigns herself to fate. To her this is the perfect answer; all rests with fate. Neither men nor gods can do anything about it. The Chinese are never religious, but superstitious. They play with religion. Fatalism is the one and only belief to which they hold whole-heartedly. It is their only salvation, it enables them to suffer everything willingly and without complaint, and it brings a stability to their emotional life in their journey through this mortal world. They are also deeply convinced that this mortal world, with its joys and sorrows, is the sum of their experience. It is here or never. The short dialogue between Tou Ngo and the executioner brings to them a sort of comradeship which is only possible in the face of Death, the common enemy of the living. And a brief memory of being with her father for a short time long ago brings a great deal of happiness to Tou Ngo in her agonizing last hour on earth.

According to Chu Ch'üan in his *Ta'i Ho Chêng Yin P'u*, Kuan Han-ch'ing wrote sixty plays; twenty only are now extant, and of these Shao Ts'êng-ch'i* maintains that only fourteen complete and three incomplete plays are authentic. Almost half of his plays have women as heroines and they belong to various classes. Considering the position of women in his time, he took a daring stand indeed in putting these heroines on the boards. Though held to be the greatest of Yüan dramatists, almost as little is known of Kuan as of the others. Even that little has engaged modern scholars in a fierce struggle to establish his identity, causing them to turn extraordinary somersaults and arrive at nowhere. Of two things they are certain: he was a native of Ta-tu and had been to Hang-chou. He was also a lyric poet of considerable stature.

CHANG BOILS THE SEA

Scholars have failed to discover any direct source from which the playwright could have drawn for this play. Frequent references of course are made in ancient Chinese literature to the daughters of dragon kings fairer than those of men. Stories of these beautiful women were much loved among the peoples of the Kin and Yüan dynasties.

A word about the Chinese dragon. This legendary animal is a fascinating creature, long and huge, and it has captured the imagination of the Chinese. Feared, worshipped and marvelled at, its virtues extolled and its viciousness decried, the dragon holds sway over China. Painters and poets sing of its grandeur, and identify themselves with it and its mighty power. The dragons are the gods who move in and out of thunder storms and control sweet rain, disastrous floods and sudden whirlwinds. Western readers must dismiss from their minds the ugly, big-bellied, fire-breathing, damsel-snatching

*'Kuan Han-ch'ing Tso P'in K'ao' ('An Inquiry into the Authenticity of the Works of Kuan Han-ch'ing'), in *Kuan Han-ch'ing Yen Chiu Lun Wên Chi* (*Studies in Kuan Han-ch'ing*), Ku Tien Wên Hsüeh Ch'u Pan Shê (Classic Literature Press), Peking, 1958, p. 112.

monster, the symbol of evil that St George and other saints rightly slew. He was a very distant cousin of the Chinese dragon, disinherited by the family long ago. Chinese emperors called themselves not only sons of Heaven but Dragons; their thrones were dragon thrones, their imperial robes dragon robes. When they were angry it was dragon anger. It symbolized everything mighty.

That the high and mighty Divine Dragon King of the Eastern Sea should have a daughter in human form to take him down a peg or two is highly amusing to the Chinese. She makes him human and pitiable. She makes him realize that he can be made powerless at times. We Chinese truly make gods after our own image, if only to make fun of them. That his daughter should fall in love with a mere human being and not with any other celestial creature, and that in the end she should turn out not to be his daughter at all after all this humiliation is the height of comedy. In the boiling sea the Dragon King's palace is destroyed, his people cooked alive and he himself left with nowhere to hide and no way out but to beg for mercy. And all for nothing.

To the Chinese love between man and woman has always been acknowledged as a debt or sin which has to be repaid or atoned for in whatsoever agonies and sorrows are requisite, and there is no end to the anxiety, heartache, ruthlessness and even cruelty to be endured till this is done. Only then will the gods appear and bring the lovers peace.

In the west Orpheus' music drew wild beasts, rocks and trees, while in ancient China if one's music could draw fish out of the depth of a pool or the sea one's musicianship had reached its zenith. I suppose they thought fish the least musical of God's creations, with an intentional dig at marine supremacy. This time it is a daughter of a royal sea dragon. She not only listens, she listens with intelligence and her interpretation is unique. She sees through the player's music-making his whole personality, and as he moves from one movement to another his mood changes and more facets of his life reveal themselves to her. This literary device has invariably become the standard but tiresome prelude to love in Chinese literature. Every wretched ancient scholar played the *ch'in*. The snapping of a string while playing is another trick worked to death by ancient Chinese literati; it signifies that something extraordinary is about to happen or is happening at the moment. The sudden death of music is chaos, a frightening experience, an omen. Music and the string and the instrument all combined have been given a life of their own, so sensitive that uninvited listening ears will stop the life of them all. Now destiny knocks and Chang immediately becomes aware of something beyond his control. He rushes out. There in front of him stands a beautiful woman, a woman to be loved. He falls head over heels in love with Ch'iung-lien at first sight. Only those who have his immortal life at heart take pity on him, the immortals Tung Hua and Mao Nü.

It is only at the moment when their earthly love is about to be consummated that they are told that all is make-believe. Everything is not what it seems. He is no son-in-law and she no daughter. They have suffered and have expiated their sin, and now they are immortals once again. All earthly things have become nothing. They have been cheated of human happiness. Are we all immortals possessing the secrets of eternal bliss, becoming mortal when we commit a sin – especially the sin of sexual love? Is it a punishment to be born a human being?

Of Li Hao-ku so little is known that even his birth-place is disputed: Pao-ting or Tung-p'ing. In one source he is said to have written four plays, in another three; anyway one only has survived. Another play of the same title by another Yüan dramatist, Shang Chung-hsien, has been lost to us.

AUTUMN IN HAN PALACE

Some twelve centuries before *Autumn in Han Palace* was written there appeared an anecdote entitled *Wang Ch'iang* in *Hsi Ching Tsa Chi* (*Miscellaneous Anecdotes of the Western Capital*) by Liu Hsin, one of the most prominent scholars of the Han dynasty (206 B.C.–A.D. 220). 'Emperor Yüan having so many wives could not visit them all, so he ordered painters to draw portraits of them, and according to the portraits he summoned them to his presence. Every one of his wives bribed the painters, some with as much as a hundred thousand pieces of gold, and none with less than fifty thousand. Only Wang Ch'iang would not: consequently she was never seen. The Hsiung-nu came to the court, and begged for a beautiful woman to be their queen. After looking through the portraits the emperor consented to let Wang Ch'iang go. The time for her departure came, and the emperor summoned her to him. Her beauty surpassed that of every one of his wives. She conversed well and had a graceful carriage. The emperor regretted his decision; however, she had been named, and prizing highly his good name abroad he did not substitute another. But without more ado he started an inquiry into the affair. The painters all fled the city, and when their private property was confiscated each was found to be worth more than ten thousand pieces of gold. Among the painters was one Mao Yen-shou of Tu-ling. He did portraits of people whether the sitter was young or old, ugly or beautiful, and the result was without fail a good likeness. Ch'ên Ch'ang of An-ling, and Liu Pai and Kung K'uan of Hsin-fêng were master-painters of oxen, horses and flying birds, but in the field of portraiture they were considered inferior to Mao Yen-shou. Yang Wang of Hsia-tu was also a skilled painter, especially in the use of colour; Fan Yü was another, well-known as a colourist. On the same day they all fled the city and scarcely one famous painter was left.' Being such an attractive story, it has appeared in numerous literary forms throughout Chinese history, and the tale of Wang Ch'iang (or Wang Chao-chün) has been enlarged, mutilated, translated and accorded other such forms of punishment as are the usual fate of many a much-loved story.

This is a slow-moving, emotional play much prized by the reading public in China. The only thing which has continued to puzzle people over the ages is that when the emperor hears of the death of Wang Ch'iang he shows not a shred of emotion for his beloved. This is singular; it has a false ring. Some again (this has come to be an awful obsession with the super-patriots) have read into the play the playwright's attack on those Chinese who surrendered themselves to the

Mongols as a woman to a man, and did not have the courage of Wang Ch'iang to choose death rather than be the queen of a foreign king.

We have a record of at least three other plays on Wang Ch'iang by other Yüan dramatists: *Chao-chün Goes by the Night Moon* by Wu Ch'ang-ling; *I Weep for Chao-chün* by Wang Shih-fu, author of *The Romance of the Western Chamber*, and *Chao-chün Crosses the North-east Frontier* by Chang Shih-ch'i. All have been lost.

Ma Chih-yüan was also a native of Ta-tu, very highly regarded by his fellow playwrights and hailed as a dramatist's dramatist; and *Autumn in Han Palace* was placed first in *Selected Yüan Plays*, with the other ninety-nine plays following. The editor must have had a special respect for it. Ma sang of the joys of the immortals and the sorrows of men, especially those of the literati, and very often in his plays we come face to face with the author. He was also a writer of lyric songs, from which we know that he had been a government official though his heart was not in his work. When he was about forty he came to the conclusion that 'I had better find a safe and convenient place where I can sit down and be idle,' and that 'the best place is the Western Village with its peace and quiet'. Eventually Ma resigned his position, devoted himself to literature and associated himself with a playwrights' guild to the end of his life. Some fourteen plays (some say twelve, some thirteen) are attributed to him; only eight have come down to us.

A STRATAGEM OF INTERLOCKING RINGS

This is a play about making use of a beautiful woman to bring about a man's downfall and death, a familiar enough scheme in life and in fiction, in China as anywhere else in the world. The play was probably written after the Chih Chih period (1321–3) and based on *San Kuo Chih P'ing Hua*, a storyteller's copy of the story of the Three Kingdoms* (Wei, A.D. 220–65; Shu-han, A.D. 221–64; Wu, A.D. 229–80). The material used here differs considerably from that of the

*Yen Tun-i, *Yüan Chü Chên I (Studies in Yüan Drama)*, vol. 2, Chung Hua Book Company, Shanghai, 1960, p. 474.

official histories and the historical novel about the same period written by another Yüan dramatist, Lo Kuan-chung. The anonymous playwright no doubt frequented storytelling halls, noticed how fascinating the story had proved, and turned out a play using the same material expecting to draw big crowds to see it. Tung Cho was the most powerful man of his time, Tiao Ch'an the most beautiful woman and Lü Pu the handsomest and bravest of men: the playwright had all the right ingredients for an exciting play – even if on reading it one allows oneself to be worried by one or two things which seem odd. Why for instance didn't Tiao Ch'an tell Wang Yün when he first rescued her that she was married to Lü Pu? And why when they were discovered to be man and wife did Lü Pu have to ask Wang Yün's pardon for their being together?

BIBLIOGRAPHY

Some other translations of Yüan plays into English:

Chêng T'ing-yü(?), *A Slave to Money*, tr. Hsien-i and Gladys Yang, in *Chinese Literature*, Peking, September 1962, pp. 53–92.

K'ang Chin-chih, *Li K'uei Carries Thorns*, tr. J. I. Crump, in *Anthology of Chinese Literature*, ed. Cyril Birch, Penguin Books, 1967.

Kuan Han-ch'ing, *Selected Plays of Kuan Han-ch'ing*, tr. Hsien-i and Gladys Yang, Foreign Languages Press, Peking, 1958.

Ma Chih-yüan, *Autumn in the Palace of Han*, tr. Donald Keene, in *Anthology of Chinese Literature*, ed. Cyril Birch, Penguin Books, 1967.

Wang Shih-fu, *The Romance of the Western Chamber*, tr. S. I. Hsiung, Methuen, 1935. *The West Chamber*, tr. Henry H. Hart, Stanford University Press, 1936.

Some studies of Yüan drama:

Crump, J. I., 'The Elements of Yüan Opera', in *Journal of Asian Studies*, vol. XVII, No. 3, 1958.

Crump, J. I., 'The Conventions and Craft of Yüan Drama', in *Journal of the American Oriental Society*, vol. 91, No. 1, January–March 1971.

Dolby, A. W. E., 'Kuan Han-ch'ing', *Asia Major*, vol. XVI, parts 1–2, 1971.

Liu, James J. Y., *Elizabethan and Yüan: A Brief Comparison of Some Conventions in Poetic Drama*, Occasional Paper No. 8, China Society, London, 1955.

Scott, A. C., *The Classical Theatre of China*, Allen and Unwin, 1957.

NOTE ON THE ILLUSTRATIONS

The illustrations to *The Soul of Ch'ien-nü Leaves Her Body* and *Chang Boils the Sea* are woodcuts by unknown artists of the period of Ch'ung Chên (1628–44) of the Ming dynasty. They originally appeared in the *Collection of Willow Branches* and were reproduced in *Yüan Jên Tsa Chü Hsüan* (*Selected Plays of the Yüan Dramatists*), ed. Ku Hsüeh-chien, Tso Chia Ch'u Pan Shê (Authors' Press), Peking, 1955. The illustrations to *The Orphan of Chao*, *The Injustice Done to Tou Ngo*, *Autumn in Han Palace* and *A Stratagem of Interlocking Rings* are reproduced here from those in *Selected Yüan Plays*, published by the Chung Hua Book Company, Shanghai. Unfortunately no mention is made there as to their origins. They were probably Ming woodcuts too, as many Ming editions of Yüan plays are well illustrated.

THE ORPHAN OF CHAO

by

Chi Chün-hsiang

(*late thirteenth century*)

THE ORPHAN OF CHAO

*CHARACTERS**

TU-AN KU, *the generalissimo*
CHAO SHUO, *the emperor's son-in-law*
PRINCESS ROYAL, *his wife*
CH'ÊNG YING, *a physician*
HAN CHÜEH, *a general*
KUNG-SUN CH'U-CHIU, *a retired official*
CH'ÊNG PO, *son to Chao Shuo and the Princess Royal*
WEI CHIANG, *an official*
CHANG CH'IEN, *servant to Wei Chiang*

SOLDIERS, *a* SPECIAL MESSENGER
and a SERVANT BOY

This play, adapted into English with some variations for radio, was translated into Swedish by my late friend Mrs Ella Byström-Bæckström of Lidingö, Sweden, and was broadcast by the Swedish Broadcasting Corporation on 4 March 1957.

*This and other lists of characters in this volume are added by the translator.

THE ORPHAN OF CHAO

THE WEDGE

Enter TU-AN KU *with* SOLDIERS.

TU-AN KU: I am Tu-an Ku, a general of the Kingdom of Tsin. Of all his many officials His Majesty trusts only two: a civil servant, Chao Tun, and an army officer, myself. There has never been any friendship lost between Chao and myself. Several times indeed I have plotted to have him killed. The problem is how to do it. For one thing Chao's son is the Emperor's son-in-law. Once I sent a strong-arm man to assassinate him, and the fellow, would you believe it, ran his head full tilt against a tree and killed himself. On another occasion while on a tour of inspection Chao saw a man dying of hunger under a mulberry tree and gave him food and wine, and the man went on his way without even saying good-bye. Sometime later the Kingdom of Tibet sent as a tribute a dog called the Supernatural Ao, which His Majesty in turn bestowed upon me. Having got this dog I thought out a plan to kill Chao. I had the dog locked up in an empty room for several days without food or water. Meanwhile in my back garden I had the figure of a man made out of straw, and on it I put a purple robe, a jade belt, an ivory tablet and a pair of black boots – exactly like the clothing worn by Chao at court. And inside the figure I hung the offal of a sheep. Then I led the dog out, ripped open Chao's purple robe and gave the dog the offal to eat. I kept up this training for three months hoping soon to make use of the trick. One day I went to see the Emperor and told him that some treacherous fellow was plotting in secret against his person. His Majesty was furious and asked me who this man was. I informed him that the tribute from Tibet, the Supernatural Ao, was endowed with foresight and would be able to reveal the identity of the man. The Emperor was delighted beyond words and asked for the dog to be brought to him. I led in the brute. At that moment Chao was standing beside His Majesty's couch. As soon as the dog saw him it pounced upon him and started to bite. The Emperor ordered me to release the dog, and when I let it go it chased Chao round and round the hall. This infuriated an officer named Hsi Mi-ming who struck the dog down and tore it in two. Once out of the palace gate Chao looked for his carriage. I had already ordered someone to take away two of his four horses, as well as one of the two wheels of his carriage, so when he got in it it wouldn't move. Suddenly from somewhere a powerful-looking man appeared. With one arm balancing the carriage and the other guiding the horses he managed to save Chao and they made their escape. Who do you think the man was? It was the one who had been dying of hunger that day under the mulberry tree. With His Majesty's consent I had the entire Chao family, some three hundred of them, put to the sword. Only Chao Shuo his son, the Emperor's son-in-law, and the Princess Royal remain alive. It is better to uproot the grass than cut it short. I have now sent a special messenger with a forged edict from the Emperor commanding Chao Shuo to take his own life by one of the three means reserved for the royal family: a bowstring, a dagger, or a cup of poisoned wine. I have ordered him to go quickly and come straight back and report. *Exit.*

Enter CHAO SHUO *and the* PRINCESS ROYAL.

CHAO SHUO: I am Chao Shuo. Attend to me, Your Royal Highness, these are my last words. You are now with child. If it is a girl no plans need be made; but if it is a boy, let him be called the Orphan of Chao. When he becomes a man he shall avenge my parents' death.

PRINCESS ROYAL [*weeps*]: This is more than I can bear!

Enter a SPECIAL MESSENGER *with followers.*

MESSENGER: I must hurry. Here is the gate of his house. [*sees* CHAO SHUO] Kneel, Chao Shuo, and listen to the Emperor's decree. Because of your family's treachery they have been put to the sword, every one of them. But a particle of treason still remains. You, since you are related to the imperial family, we could not bring ourself to hand over to the executioner. Instead we offer you the three imperial punishments: choose one and die. The Princess Royal will be held prisoner in this house, entirely cut off from her family. Chao Shuo, this is the Emperor's sacred decree, not to be delayed or disobeyed. Decide and act quickly.

CHAO SHUO: What is to be done, Your Royal Highness?

My loyalty to the Emperor has been ill-spent,
suddenly it comes to nothing.
That traitor gnawing wormlike at the state wields all the power.

PRINCESS ROYAL: Heaven, have pity! He is so cruel that we shall die and not even have graves to receive us.

CHAO SHUO:

Not even a burial in our family vault!

Remember well what I have charged you with, Your Royal Highness.

PRINCESS ROYAL: I understand.

CHAO SHUO:

> Tears like rain flow down my cheeks,
> Another word, another sorrow.

CHAO SHUO *stabs himself and dies.*

PRINCESS ROYAL: My lord! Oh, my heart is breaking! *Exit.*

MESSENGER: Chao Shuo has killed himself with a dagger and the Princess Royal is now confined to the house. I must go back and report to my master. *Exeunt.*

ACT ONE

Enter TU-AN KU.

TU-AN KU: My one fear now is that the Princess Royal may give birth to a son, and this son will grow up to become my enemy. By now she should have given birth to her child. How is it that the messenger I sent is still not back?

Enter a SOLDIER.

SOLDIER: I beg to report to Your Excellency, the Princess has given birth to a son, and she calls him the Orphan of Chao.

TU-AN KU: Indeed! Calls him the Orphan of Chao? Well, we can bide our time. A month will be soon enough to kill the child. Bear my orders to General Han Chüeh. Tell him to keep guard at the gates of the house. No precautions need be taken with those going in, but all those coming out must be searched. Anyone attempting to smuggle out the Orphan of Chao will have his whole family put to the sword, not one member of his nine generations shall be spared. At the same time see that notice of this is put up all round, so that all officers know that no one is to disregard these orders or he himself will pay the penalty. *Exeunt.*

Enter the PRINCESS ROYAL *carrying a baby.*

PRINCESS ROYAL:

All the sorrows of man
Are gathered in my heart,
Like the rain of an autumn night
Each drop a note of grief.

I cannot forget what my husband said before he died. But Heaven, how am I to get this child out of the house! I haven't a single member of my family left now, only an old retainer called Ch'êng Ying. When he comes I have a plan I must lay before him.

Enter CH'ÊNG YING *with a medicine chest slung over his shoulders.*

CH'ÊNG YING: I am Ch'êng Ying. I used to be a village physician until the Emperor's son-in-law took me into his protection. He has always treated me with the greatest favour, more so than his other retainers. Now it is I who wait on the Princess Royal, carrying her tea and her meals to her each day. Her Royal Highness has recently given birth to a son. But I fear for him: he cannot escape the wicked Tu-an Ku. A vain hope! Her Royal Highness has sent for me. I expect she wants some medicine after her confinement. Here's the gate, I'll go straight in. [*sees the* PRINCESS ROYAL] Your Royal Highness has sent for me. What is your wish?

PRINCESS ROYAL: What bitter fate has overtaken our family! Ch'êng Ying, this was the reason I sent for you. You have always been part of our household and have not been ill-treated, I think. This child that has been born to me, whom his father as he was dying called the Orphan of Chao, can you find a way of hiding him and taking him secretly out of the house? Then when he comes of age, let him avenge the Chao family.

CH'ÊNG YING: Don't you know, Your Royal Highness, that the wicked Tu-an Ku has heard of the birth of your child and had notices posted at the four city gates saying that anyone who helps the Orphan will be put to death, together with the nine generations of his family.

PRINCESS ROYAL [*kneels*]: Take pity on the three hundred dead souls of the Chao family whose vengeance depends upon this child.

CH'ÊNG YING: Please get up, Your Royal Highness! What if I take the child away and Tu-an Ku comes to know of it and asks you for the child, and you say you have given him to Ch'êng Ying? If my family are all to die, so be it; but this child will not live either.

PRINCESS ROYAL: Very well, very well, very well. You shall leave this house in peace, Ch'êng Ying. His father killed himself with a dagger – [*takes the cord from her skirt*] Very well, very well. Let his mother follow him! *Exit.*

CH'ÊNG YING: The Princess Royal has hanged herself. I dare not stay any longer. I'll open this medicine chest, put the child into it and cover it with herbs. Heaven, have pity! Well, if I can save you, child, by smuggling you out, fortune must be with you and I shall have done well. And if you're discovered, it'll be the end of you, and the death of all my family as well. *Exit.*

Enter HAN CHÜEH *with* SOLDIERS.

HAN CHÜEH: I am Han Chüeh, general under Tu-an Ku.

Wind and rain are in their season and the year at peace.
That such a man as Tu-an Ku should be in favour!
The loyal and dutiful beheaded in the market square,
The false and treacherous secure in the palace.
Now his one aim is to intimidate the people,
Those who opposed him have long since been swept away.
In a word, he is the cruellest of men.

When will it end, this bitter enmity between the families of Tu-an and Chao?

One day you will anger Heaven above
And inflame the people below.
Does it hold no fear for you, the clamour of ten thousand mouths?
Even Heaven will show its fiercest face, forgiving none
But visiting its wrath if not on you, upon your sons and grandsons after you.
You villain, between Chao Tun and I
Is a fellowship of twenty years to mean no loyalty?

Tell those at the gate to let me know when anyone goes out.

SOLDIER: Yes, sir.

Enter CH'ÊNG YING *nervously.*

CH'ÊNG YING: I am glad that General Han is on duty at the gate. My master's father helped to promote him. If I can make my way past, the child's life and mine will be saved.

CH'ÊNG YING *goes out of the gates.*

HAN CHÜEH: Bring back that man with the medicine chest. Who are you?

CH'ÊNG YING: I am a village physician. My name is Ch'êng Ying.

HAN CHÜEH: Where have you come from?

CH'ÊNG YING: I have been preparing some medicine in the house of the Princess Royal.

HAN CHÜEH: What medicine?

CH'ÊNG YING: Some tonic for Her Royal Highness.

HAN CHÜEH: What have you got in that chest?

CH'ÊNG YING: Herbs.

HAN CHÜEH: What herbs?

CH'ÊNG YING: *Chieh keng* for coughs, liquorice root, peppermint and others.

HAN CHÜEH: What else have you got hidden there?

CH'ÊNG YING: I haven't anything hidden there.

HAN CHÜEH: Very well, go along. [CH'ÊNG YING *goes.*] Ch'êng Ying, come back. What have you got in that chest?

CH'ÊNG YING: Herbs.

HAN CHÜEH: What else have you got hidden there?

CH'ÊNG YING: I haven't anything hidden there.

HAN CHÜEH: Go along then. [CH'ÊNG YING *goes.*] Ch'êng Ying, come back. You must have something mysterious hidden there. When I let you go, you go like an arrow from the string of a bow; but when I call you back, you come like a piece of fur dragged over a rug. Do you think I don't know you?

An honoured guest you are in the house of Chao Tun,
And I a soldier sworn to Tu-an Ku.
You have hidden the young offspring not yet a month old.

Ch'êng Ying, am I not right?

How will you leave this tigers' den where not a breath
of air can escape?
But I am not an officer of the baser breed,
I shall not have you cross-examined.

Ch'êng Ying, I imagine you have received many favours from the Chao family?

CH'ÊNG YING: Yes. Needless to say I know what kindness is and I will repay it.

HAN CHÜEH [*to his* SOLDIERS]: Leave us. Come if I call; otherwise stay out of sight. [*Exeunt* SOLDIERS. HAN CHÜEH *opens the medicine chest.*] You said there was *chieh keng* for coughs, liquorice root and peppermint, but I have found a mandrake. [CH'ÊNG *falls at his feet.*]

With bright shining little eyes he tries to make me out,
So quiet in the chest he seems to swallow every sound,
So tightly bundled he can scarcely stretch his legs,
So narrow how can he even turn onto his side?
These are not the conditions for becoming a man;
Indeed becoming a man is not to be his condition.

CH'ÊNG YING: Don't be angry with me, Your Honour. Listen to what your servant has to say and I will tell you everything. Her Royal Highness has hanged herself. She charged me to protect the child so that when he grows up he can look after the family graveyard. Happily we have met Your Honour and earnestly hope you will help us. If this child is killed it will mean the end of the entire Chao family.

HAN CHÜEH: If I were to hand over this child, I would have honours and riches all the days of my life, would I not? But

I, Han Chüeh, am a man. How could I do such a thing! Take the child and go. If Tu-an Ku should ask, I'll answer for it.

CH'ÊNG YING: I thank you, general.

CH'ÊNG YING takes up the chest and goes, but comes back to kneel before HAN CHÜEH.

HAN CHÜEH: When I say I let you go, do you think I'm playing with you, Ch'êng Ying? Go, and go quickly!

CH'ÊNG YING: Thank you, general, thank you.

He goes, comes back again, and kneels down.

HAN CHÜEH: How is it you've come back again?

Since you lack the courage,
Who forces you to be the orphan's guardian?
Don't you know that loyal subjects are not afraid of death?
Those who are afraid of death are not loyal subjects.

CH'ÊNG YING: When once we are outside the gate, general, you will report to Tu-an Ku. He will have another officer sent to arrest me and the child won't have the slightest chance of surviving. Arrest me and have yourself rewarded. The orphan and I are willing to die together.

HAN CHÜEH: Can you not set your mind at rest and go?

What kinship do I claim with Tu-an Ku?
You are loyal: I too am a man of my word.
If you are willing to sacrifice your life,
I too am willing to give mine.
Take the orphan and hide him deep in the mountain.
There train him till he comes of age,
And school him in the arts of peace and war,
So that one day he shall command the army,

Seize that villain,
Break his head and tear him limb from limb,
To avenge the souls of all his dead.
Then we shall not have kicked against the door of justice
Or shouldered the burden of danger and hardship in vain.

Go in peace, Ch'êng Ying.

Far better for Tu-an Ku to come and seek an explanation.
But you, be diligent in your care for him morning and night,
Until the child shall come of age.
Then tell him what happened long ago;
Be sure to teach him to take vengeance
And not forget me, his great benefactor.

HAN CHÜEH *cuts his own throat.*

CH'ÊNG YING: Ah! General Han has killed himself. What's to be done? I fear the other officers will discover it and report to Tu-an Ku. The orphan and I must run for our lives. *Exeunt.*

ACT TWO

Enter TU-AN KU *with* SOLDIERS.

TU-AN KU: The Orphan of Chao! Can he have vanished into thin air! Why haven't they brought me the child yet? I am worried. Someone go to the gate and look.

Enter a SOLDIER.

SOLDIER: Calamity on calamity, general.

TU-AN KU: What do you mean?

SOLDIER: The Princess Royal has hanged herself and General Han who was on guard at the gate has taken his own life as well.

TU-AN KU: Why should General Han kill himself? The orphan must have escaped. What shall I do? I have it! I'll forge a royal decree and have all the newborn children between one month and six months old collected up and killed. The Orphan of Chao is bound to be among them. Come, have proclamations sent out. *Exeunt.*

Enter KUNG-SUN CH'U-CHIU *with his* SERVANT BOY.

KUNG-SUN CH'U-CHIU: I am Kung-sun Ch'u-chiu. I was an official of the middle rank under the Emperor. But I am old now, and once I had seen that Tu-an Ku had taken all power in the kingdom into his own hands I found it impossible to do my job. In the end I was dismissed. Now I am a farmer with a thatched cottage, several acres of land and a hoe to help me, here in the village of T'ai-p'ing.

Once I slept in a small tent listening to the cold bugle blow;
Now I lean at a poor cottage door counting the wild geese fly by.
If I had not drawn back my feet from the torrents,
I might well have had my head shorn in the market-place.

Enter CH'ÊNG YING.

CH'ÊNG YING: I am so frightened! With death dogging my steps I have managed to get out of the city. I've heard that Tu-an Ku has had all the children in the Kingdom of Tsin between one month and six months old gathered together into the general's headquarters and he will probably kill every one of them himself. Where am I going to take this child? Ah, now I remember – Kung-sun Ch'u-chiu in T'ai-p'ing village. He and Chao were on excellent terms with each other when they were both at court. He is an honest and straightforward old gentleman and I can hide the orphan there. Here is the village now. I shall put the medicine chest under this shed. Rest here for a while, little one. When I've seen Kung-sun Ch'u-chiu I'll come back to you. Boy! go and announce that Ch'êng Ying begs to see the master.

BOY: There's someone called Ch'êng Ying at the gate.

KUNG-SUN CH'U-CHIU: Ask him to come in.

BOY: Please come in.

KUNG-SUN CH'U-CHIU: What has brought you here, Ch'êng Ying?

CH'ÊNG YING: I knew you lived in T'ai-p'ing village so I have come especially to pay you a visit.

KUNG-SUN CH'U-CHIU: How are all my colleagues at court since my dismissal?

CH'ÊNG YING: Alas, things can't be compared with the time Your Honour was at court. Now that Tu-an Ku has scraped all the power into his own hands, nothing is quite as before.

KUNG-SUN CH'U-CHIU: All the ministers and officials should remonstrate with the Emperor.

CH'ÊNG YING: Your Honour, there have been treacherous ministers and officials since olden times. Even in the days of the wisest kings there existed four extremely evil men.

KUNG-SUN CH'U-CHIU:

Who can be likened to this man
Whom ten thousand hate and thousands loathe
And only one esteems?

Whose only talent was to wipe out the whole family
of Chao.

CH'ÊNG YING: Luckily nothing escapes the eyes of Heaven. The Chao family has not been completely wiped out.

KUNG-SUN CH'U-CHIU: More than three hundred of their number were slaughtered, the Emperor's son-in-law stabbed himself, the Princess Royal hanged herself. Who can be left?

CH'ÊNG YING: The Princess Royal gave birth to a son. It is he who is left. But we are afraid Tu-an Ku will come to know of it and want to kill him too, and if this little one were killed, then won't it indeed be true that the whole family has been wiped out.

KUNG-SUN CH'U-CHIU: Where is the orphan now? I wonder if someone has saved him and brought him away.

CH'ÊNG YING: Since Your Honour takes pity on the Chao family I shall be bold and tell you the truth. Before she took her life the Princess Royal entrusted the child to me, charging me to take care of him until he was of age to avenge his parents. When I brought him to the gate General Han Chüeh let us pass, then cut his throat and killed himself. I have nowhere to hide the orphan, so I have come especially to you, Your Honour. I understand you and Chao Tun were both at court at the same time, and were on intimate terms with each other. Have pity, and save this child.

KUNG-SUN CH'U-CHIU: Where is the orphan now?

CH'ÊNG YING: At present under the shed outside.

KUNG-SUN CH'U-CHIU: Don't frighten the child. Bring him in quickly.

CH'ÊNG YING *brings in the chest, opens it and looks in.*

CH'ÊNG YING: Thank Heaven, the little one is still asleep. Your Honour, I am almost forty-five, and I have a son born not a month ago. It is my plan to pass my child off as the Orphan of Chao. I do this for two reasons: to repay the Emperor's son-in-law for his kindness to me, and to save the lives of the rest of the children of Tsin. Your Honour must go to Tu-an Ku and simply report to him that the Orphan of Chao is hidden with Ch'êng Ying. Let him kill us, father and son. Then Your Honour can devote your time to bringing up the orphan, and when he comes of age he can avenge his parents. This is the best plan, don't you think?

KUNG-SUN CH'U-CHIU: How old are you, Ch'êng Ying?

CH'ÊNG YING: Forty-five.

KUNG-SUN CH'U-CHIU: It will take twenty years before the little one is able to avenge his parents. If you live another twenty years you will be only sixty-five. If I live another twenty years, that will make me ninety, will it not? Whether I shall be alive or dead then who can say, but how am I going to be able to see the Chao family avenged? You say you are willing to sacrifice your son, Ch'êng Ying. Instead, leave your son with me. You go and tell Tu-an Ku that Kung-sun Ch'u-chiu has the orphan hidden in the village of T'ai-p'ing. This will be the better plan.

CH'ÊNG YING: This may sound the better plan, Your Honour, but how can I put you in such a position? Pass off my child as the orphan and tell Tu-an Ku, and let father and son die together.

KUNG-SUN CH'U-CHIU: I am determined. No more hesitation, Ch'êng Ying.

CH'ÊNG YING: No, no. Your Honour is still in the prime of life.

KUNG-SUN CH'U-CHIU:

> My vigour cannot be compared with former days:
> I may not last another beating of the evening drum
> Or another striking of the morning bell.

CH'ÊNG YING: You lead a life of ease and comfort in your home, and I who know no better suddenly descend upon you and implicate you in this unhappy affair! How can I forgive myself!

KUNG-SUN CH'U-CHIU: What are you saying, Ch'êng Ying? I am already seventy. Death is an everyday affair to me. I shall not quarrel with it whether it comes early or late.

> When I contemplate this puppet stage manipulated by the sounds of drum and flute,
> I look on it as no more than a short dream I have dreamed.
> Suddenly when I look back I am too old for noble deeds.
> How shall I meet my benefactors if a kindness can't be repaid?
> How can I ignore a duty and expect to be called brave?

CH'ÊNG YING: You have promised, Your Honour. You won't go back on your word?

KUNG-SUN CH'U-CHIU:

> Why give a promise and not give it in good faith?

CH'ÊNG YING: If you succeed in saving the Orphan of Chao your name will go down in history and be remembered for all generations.

KUNG-SUN CH'U-CHIU:

> There is no need to pay me compliments,

A man should not be anxious for the end of his life,
And already my hair has grown scanty and white.

CH'ÊNG YING: There is one thing more, Your Honour. When Tu-an Ku arrests you, how will you bear it when they put you to the torture? You are bound to give me away. If father and son are to die, so be it. But how pitiful it would be if the Orphan of Chao had to die in spite of all your suffering.

KUNG-SUN CH'U-CHIU: Set your mind at rest, Ch'êng Ying.

Once given my word weighs a thousand pieces of gold.
Were I sent to climb mountains of daggers and peaks of swords,
Whatever I began I would finish.

When an old man dies it is not even worth mentioning.

CH'ÊNG YING: Then we must hurry. I shall take the orphan back to my home and bring my child here to T'ai-p'ing village. *Exeunt.*

ACT THREE

Enter TU-AN KU *with* SOLDIERS.

TU-AN KU: How could the orphan have escaped! I have had a public proclamation put out that if the Orphan of Chao is not delivered to me within three days all the children in my headquarters will be killed. Someone go to the gate and see if there is anyone coming with any information. If so, report to me at once.

Enter CH'ÊNG YING.

CH'ÊNG YING: Go and report that I have news of the whereabouts of the Orphan of Chao.

SOLDIER: You stay here while I report to the general. Sir, someone has come with news of the Orphan of Chao.

TU-AN KU: Where is he?

SOLDIER: At the gate.

TU-AN KU: Tell him to come here.

SOLDIER: Come here.

TU-AN KU: You, fellow, who are you?

CH'ÊNG YING: I am a village physician. My name is Ch'êng Ying.

TU-AN KU: Where is the Orphan of Chao?

CH'ÊNG YING: He is hidden in T'ai-p'ing village, in the home of Kung-sun Ch'u-chiu.

TU-AN KU: How do you know?

CH'ÊNG YING: Kung-sun Ch'u-chiu is an acquaintance of mine. I went to visit him the other day. In his room there lay a baby. Kung-sun is seventy and never had any children, and I wondered where this child had come from. When I asked him was this little thing the Orphan of Chao, I saw plainly that his colour changed instantly and he wasn't able to answer. It is this that makes me certain the Orphan of Chao is at Kung-sun's house.

TU-AN KU: Tut, tut, fellow, I'm not that easily taken in! There has never been any enmity between you and Kung-sun. Why should you say he has hidden the Orphan of Chao? Are you sure that you know what you're doing? If what you've said is true, the end is in sight. If what you've said is not true, then someone sharpen their sword and off with his head at once!

CH'ÊNG YING: Don't be angry, Your Excellency. Please listen to me. Indeed there is no enmity between Kung-sun and myself. I only do this because of your proclamation and because you say you will kill all the children in your headquarters. I want to save the children. And there is another reason too. I am forty-five and my wife has just given birth to a son who's not yet a month old, and we've been forced to hand him over. But if my child dies, my whole family will die with him. And I know if you have the Orphan of Chao the children of the kingdom will be spared and nothing will happen to my son. It's for this reason I have come to inform.

TU-AN KU [*smiles*]: Ah, true. Kung-sun and Chao Tun were fellow officials at court. It's understandable that this should happen. I shall order soldiers to accompany Ch'êng Ying and myself to T'ai-p'ing village this very day and have Kung-sun Ch'u-chiu arrested. *Exeunt.*

Enter KUNG-SUN CH'U-CHIU.

KUNG-SUN CH'U-CHIU: Sooner or later that scoundrel Tu-an Ku is bound to come.

I see a cloud of warlike dust flying the bridge across the stream.
It must be them, that horde of murderers of the loyal and good;
Soldiers in battle array deployed in perfect rank,
Their swords and lances sparkling in a line.
I see the time has come for me to die today,
Nor shall I escape the punishment of a beating from their rods.

Enter TU-AN KU, CH'ÊNG YING *and* SOLDIERS.

TU-AN KU: Surround T'ai-p'ing village. Which is Kung-sun's house, Ch'êng Ying?

CH'ÊNG YING: That is the one.

TU-AN KU: Bring the old fellow here. Kung-sun Ch'u-chiu, did you know that you are guilty of a crime?

KUNG-SUN CH'U-CHIU: I did not know, and I am guilty of no crime.

TU-AN KU: I know that you and Chao Tun were at court at the same time. How dare you hide the Orphan of Chao?

KUNG-SUN CH'U-CHIU: How dare I hide the orphan, general?

TU-AN KU: There's no confession without a beating! Someone take a thick rod and beat him hard.

A SOLDIER *beats* KUNG-SUN CH'U-CHIU.

KUNG-SUN CH'U-CHIU:

I remember when I was dismissed and bade farewell to court,
I made a bond of everlasting friendship with Chao Tun.

Who has been telling you all this?

TU-AN KU: Ch'êng Ying. He has informed against you.

KUNG-SUN CH'U-CHIU: You've murdered the whole Chao family. Only this child is left, and now you wish to kill him too.

Truly you are like a hurricane pouncing on the eagle at will,
Like a hard frost bent on striking at the withered root of grass.

TU-AN KU: You, old fellow, where have you hidden the orphan? Tell me the truth at once if you don't wish to be beaten.

KUNG-SUN CH'U-CHIU: What orphan have I hidden? Who has seen it?

TU-AN KU: You won't confess? Someone beat him hard.

A SOLDIER *beats* KUNG-SUN CH'U-CHIU.

You stubborn old carcase, will you not confess! The devil take you! [*to* CH'ÊNG YING] You informed against him, Ch'êng Ying. You take a rod and beat him.

CH'ÊNG YING: I am only a village physician, general. My wrist is too weak even to mix herbs. How am I to manage a rod to beat someone?

TU-AN KU: You'll not beat him because you're afraid he might let out that you're his accomplice.

CH'ÊNG YING: I'll beat him, general.

CH'ÊNG YING *fumbles among the rods.*

TU-AN KU: Look at you! lifting up one rod after another and then choosing a thin one. You're afraid that when you beat him and he begins to feel the pain, he'll say that you have a part in this too.

CH'ÊNG YING: I'll take a thick one to beat him.

TU-AN KU: Stop! First you choose a thin rod, now you choose a thick one. With two or three strokes of this you'll have killed him. And you'll be killing the only witness against you.

CH'ÊNG YING: When I chose a thin rod you said it wouldn't do; when I choose a thick one, you say that won't do either. You are making it very difficult for me.

TU-AN KU: You only need take a middle-sized rod for beating Kung-sun. You, old fellow, did you know it's Ch'êng Ying who's going to beat you now?

CH'ÊNG YING *raises the rod.*

CH'ÊNG YING: Now confess!

CH'ÊNG YING *beats* KUNG-SUN CH'U-CHIU *three times.*

KUNG-SUN CH'U-CHIU: Ah, aah! I've been beaten before

but none of the strokes were as painful as these. Who is it that's beating me?

TU-AN KU: Ch'êng Ying.

KUNG-SUN CH'U-CHIU: You, Ch'êng Ying? How is it *you*'re beating me?

CH'ÊNG YING: The beating has made the old fellow talk nonsense, general.

KUNG-SUN CH'U-CHIU:

> Cruel Ch'êng Ying, what enmity is there between us,
> That you make me, old Kung-sun, suffer this outrage?

CH'ÊNG YING: Confess, and be quick!

KUNG-SUN CH'U-CHIU: I'll confess, I'll confess.

CH'ÊNG YING *grows agitated.*

> Stealing a glance at Ch'êng Ying,
> I see he is so frightened his knees are already trembling.

CH'ÊNG YING: Confess now this instant, if you don't wish to be beaten to death.

KUNG-SUN CH'U-CHIU: I will, I will, I will.

> We two conspired to save this little child.

TU-AN KU: I knew you would talk in the end. You said there were two of you. You are one; who is the other? Speak the truth and I'll spare your life.

KUNG-SUN CH'U-CHIU: You wish me to name the other. I'll name him, I'll name him.

> Ah, the name has just slipped from the tip of my tongue.

TU-AN KU: You have some part in this, Ch'êng Ying, haven't you?

CH'ÊNG YING [*to* KUNG-SUN CH'U-CHIU]: Old fellow, don't you dare accuse an innocent man.

KUNG-SUN CH'U-CHIU: What are you so afraid of, Ch'êng Ying?

TU-AN KU: Just a moment ago you said there were two of you, now you say there's no one else?

KUNG-SUN CH'U-CHIU:

> I have been beaten so hard I don't know my head
> from my heels.

TU-AN KU: Will you still not tell? I'll have you beaten to death, old fellow.

KUNG-SUN CH'U-CHIU:

> If you beat me till my skin is in shreds,
> My flesh completely stripped away,
> Do not expect one word from me to incriminate
> another.

Enter a SOLDIER *carrying a baby.*

SOLDIER: General, the day is yours. I have found the Orphan of Chao in a cave.

TU-AN KU [*smiles*]: Bring the little brat nearer to me. I'll kill it myself. You say there's no Orphan of Chao here – but what is this? It makes my blood boil merely to see the child. Just let me draw my sword. There! there! there! [CH'ÊNG YING *gestures in agony.*] Isn't this the moment I've longed for all my life!

KUNG-SUN CH'U-CHIU:

> Ah,
> To see the infant lying in a pool of blood
> I tremble and shudder,

Today no more than ten days old.
When the sword thrust how he must have begged to be spared.

CH'ÊNG YING *hides his tears.*

I see it is like boiling oil poured on the heart of Ch'êng Ying,
Yet he dare not let his tears fall before all.

You villain, Tu-an Ku, take care! There is still Heaven above. And how will Heaven forgive you? My death is nothing.

At seventy I cannot be said to be too old to die;
Were it one year old this child were still too young.
I charge you, Ch'êng Ying, who will live after us,
Not to forget the untimely death of Chao Shuo.
Tell everyone time passes fast
And vengeance for such wrongs comes soon.
Have that villain chopped into a thousand pieces!

Now let me dash my head against the steps and die. *Exit.*

Enter a SOLDIER.

SOLDIER: Kung-sun has dashed his head against the steps and died.

TU-AN KU [*smiles*]: Well, if the old fellow's dashed himself to death, that's an end of it! Ch'êng Ying, you deserve all the credit for this. If it hadn't been for you, how would I have been able to kill the orphan?

CH'ÊNG YING: I bear the Chao family no grudge. I only did it because if we hadn't found the orphan, my own child would not have lived.

TU-AN KU: You are truly a friend in need. You shall be one

of my retainers. And I shall help your child to grow up to be someone of importance. You can teach him literature and the arts and I shall give him his military training. You know I too am near fifty and haven't an heir. I shall adopt your child. I am getting on in years. All my official titles will be there waiting for him to inherit afterwards. What do you say?

CH'ÊNG YING: This is a great honour, general, and I don't know how to thank you.

TU-AN KU:

It was only when Chao Tun alone shone at court
I couldn't help my anger being roused.
Now I've succeeded in nipping this bud,
There'll never be any more cause for a feud. *Exeunt.*

ACT FOUR

Enter TU-AN KU *with* SOLDIERS.

TU-AN KU: It is twenty years already since I killed the Orphan of Chao. I have adopted Ch'êng Ying's son and taught him the eighteen branches of the military arts. Whatever he does, he does well. His archery and horsemanship are superior to mine. With the prowess and ability of this child in mind I have long had my plans mapped out. I shall put the Emperor to death and seize his throne, and the boy shall take over all my present positions. Nothing less than this will truly satisfy my hopes. He has gone to the parade ground to practise his horsemanship and archery. When he comes back I'll consult with him. *Exit.*

Enter CH'ÊNG YING *with a scroll in his hand.*

CH'ÊNG YING:

Sun and moon hasten the advance of age,
Time hurries the young.
There is endless matter in my heart,
But I dare not speak out fully.

How fast time goes! It is twenty years since I came to live in the family of Tu-an Ku. What does Tu-an Ku know of the real story? Even the child has no idea. I am sixty-five this year. If anything should happen to me, who is to tell the boy he should avenge his family? Between hesitation and anxiety I have been kept awake night and day. Now I have had this scroll drawn with the portraits of those loyal officials and brave soldiers long ago who died an untimely death. If the boy should ask me about them, I shall tell him their stories one by one. I'll sit here in the study and wait for him to come back, and then see what's to be done.

Enter CH'ÊNG PO.

CH'ÊNG PO: I am Ch'êng Po. My father Ch'êng Ying lives on this side, my adopted father Tu-an Ku on the other. In the day I train at the military arts, and at night I study the classics. I am going to see my father.

I wait on the noble Emperor Ling of Tsin,
And assist the worthy minister Tu-an Ku.
With my skills in the arts of peace and war
I could face ten thousand enemies.

CH'ÊNG YING: I've spread out this scroll of paintings. What tragedies they show! For the Orphan of Chao's sake how many worthy officials, how many honourable men sacrificed their lives – my own child too.

CH'ÊNG PO: Come, take my horse. Where is my father?

SOLDIER: In the study.

CH'ÊNG PO: Send someone to announce me.

SOLDIER: Ch'êng Po has come.

CH'ÊNG YING: Send him in.

SOLDIER: Please go in.

CH'ÊNG PO: I am back from the parade ground.

CH'ÊNG YING: Go and have your meal.

CH'ÊNG PO: Now I am outside the door. Usually when my father sees me he is happy. But today when he saw me come, he was worried and tearful. I don't know what to make of it. I'll go in and ask him. Who has insulted you, father? Tell me. I'll make sure he won't get away with it.

CH'ÊNG YING: If I were to tell you the whole story, not even your own parents could advise you what to do. Go and have your meal. [*weeps*]

CH'ÊNG PO: I simply don't understand what you mean.

Why the hidden tears?

CH'ÊNG YING *sighs.*

Why the long sigh?

I am here, father. If no one has insulted you,

Have you exchanged cross words?

CH'ÊNG YING: Stay here in the study for a while. Find something to read. I am going into the inner hall. I will be back in a moment.

CH'ÊNG YING *puts down the scroll and withdraws.*

CH'ÊNG PO: So he has left this scroll for me to look at. Let me open it and see. How strange! Here is a picture of a man in red leading an evil-looking dog. Now the dog is attacking a man dressed in purple. Another man kills the dog with an iron ball and chain. Here is a man lifting up a carriage and the carriage has only one wheel. And now this man has dashed himself to death against a tree. What stories do these tell? There are no names. Let me go on. Here is a general with a bowstring, a cup of poisoned wine and a dagger before him. He kills himself with the dagger. Now this general takes a sword and cuts his own throat. Here is a physician kneeling with his hand on a medicine chest. And here a woman holding a child as though she were entrusting it to the physician. Ah, she too takes her own life. How pitiful! How ruthless the man in red is! Here he has an old man with a white beard brutally beaten. I wonder whether this family has any connection with mine?

If I do not kill this villain I am not a man,
I am not afraid to face him and demand revenge.
Whose kinsmen can these be in this pool of blood?
Whose ancestors those beheaded in the market square?

I am completely mystified. I'll wait till my father comes back and ask him what it all means.

CH'ÊNG YING *comes forward.*

CH'ÊNG YING: I've been listening a long time to what you've been saying.
CH'ÊNG PO: Will you tell me what this is all about?
CH'ÊNG YING: You want me to tell you the story of these pictures. In a way they concern you.
CH'ÊNG PO: Then tell me everything in detail, sir.
CH'ÊNG YING: Listen, Ch'êng Po, it is a very long story. The man in red and the man in purple were in fact officials in the same court. For some reason they clashed, and became enemies. For a long time the man in red had the idea that

whoever struck the first blow in combat gained the upper hand, and whoever struck last deserved to lose. So secretly he sent an assassin to do away with the man in purple. But the assassin, knowing the man in purple to be perfectly loyal and without the least trace of self-interest, realized that if he murdered him he would be offending against Heaven, and that if he went back to the man in red without carrying out the deed, his own death was certain. So that night he dashed his head against an ash-tree and died.

CH'ÊNG PO: This one who dashed his head against an ash-tree was the assassin?

CH'ÊNG YING: Yes, indeed. Now once, while on a tour of inspection, the man in purple saw a man lying on his back under a mulberry tree with his mouth wide open. He asked the man what he was doing, and the man said that his name was Ling Che and that he needed a peck of rice at each meal, but his master hadn't been able to feed him and had dismissed him. If he picked berries from the mulberry tree people would accuse him of stealing; so he lay there on his back, and if the berries fell into his mouth he would eat them; if they did not he would rather die than receive insult from others. The man in purple saw that this was a man of principle and gave him food and wine.

CH'ÊNG PO: The hungry man under the mulberry tree was Ling Che?

CH'ÊNG YING: Yes, remember it, Ch'êng Po. Then one day the Kingdom of Tibet sent as a tribute a dog called the Supernatural Ao, four feet tall. The Emperor gave it to the man in red at the time when he was planning to kill the man in purple. He had a straw figure made and dressed exactly like the man in purple and in the belly of the straw figure he hung the offal of a sheep. Then he starved the dog for several days and afterwards ripped open the straw figure and fed the dog with the offal. He did this for a hundred days. Then he went to the Emperor saying that there was a treacherous official in the court intending to do His Majesty harm. The Emperor asked where the man was, and the man in red answered that the supernatural dog which His Majesty had given him would be able to reveal the traitor. The man in red led the dog in. The man in purple was standing in the hall at the time, and the supernatural dog, taking him to be the straw figure, immediately pounced on him. The man in purple was chased round and round the hall, till an officer, angered by this, raised his iron ball and chain and struck the dog down.

CH'ÊNG PO: So this evil dog was called the Supernatural Ao.

CH'ÊNG YING: When the man in purple got out of the palace gate and mounted his carriage he did not know that two of his four horses and one of the two wheels had been taken away on the orders of the man in red. The carriage would not move. From near by a man came forward to lift one end of the axle with one arm and guide the horses with the other. His clothes were rubbed to the skin; his skin was rubbed to the bone; the bone was rubbed till the marrow could be seen. But they made good their escape. Who do you think this man was? He was the one who had once lain starving under the mulberry tree.

CH'ÊNG PO: I remember. The man in red, father, what was his name?

CH'ÊNG YING: I have forgotten, Ch'êng Po.

CH'ÊNG PO: And the man in purple, what was his name?

CH'ÊNG YING: The man in purple was once the prime minister Chao Tun. He was related to you.

CH'ÊNG PO: I had heard that there was once a prime minister Chao Tun, but I hadn't thought much about it.

CH'ÊNG YING: Now, Ch'êng Po, remember well what I am going to tell you. The man in red put to the sword the entire family of Chao Tun except for one son, Chao Shuo, the Emperor's son-in-law. The man in red forged a decree from His Majesty ordering him to choose one of the three means reserved to the royal family and take his own life. At that time the Princess Royal was expecting a child. Chao Shuo charged her that if she gave birth to a boy she should call him the Orphan of Chao and should have him avenge the death of the three hundred members of their family. After Chao Shuo's death the man in red had the Princess imprisoned in her house. When the boy was born and the news reached the man in red he at once sent General Han Chüeh to keep watch at the gate with express orders to prevent the child being smuggled out of the house. Now the Princess had a trusted retainer in her household, a country physician by the name of Ch'êng Ying.

CH'ÊNG PO: Was that you, then, father?

CH'ÊNG YING: There are many in this world who bear the same name. This was another Ch'êng Ying. Having entrusted the child to this other Ch'êng Ying, the Princess hanged herself. Ch'êng Ying took the child, but when he came to the gate of the house he was confronted by General Han who searched him and discovered the child. Ch'êng Ying pleaded with him; whereupon General Han drew his sword and killed himself.

CH'ÊNG PO: This was the General Han who killed himself for the sake of the orphan? What a good man! I shall always remember his name was Han Chüeh.

CH'ÊNG YING: Yes, this was Han Chüeh. When the man in

red heard of this he had all the children in the kingdom between one month and six months old gathered into his headquarters. He intended to kill every one of them, imagining that the Orphan of Chao was bound to be among them.

CH'ÊNG PO: How ruthless he was, the man in red!

CH'ÊNG YING: This Ch'êng Ying also had a child that was not yet a month old, and this child he passed off as the Orphan of Chao and took to the village of T'ai-p'ing, to a certain Kung-sun Ch'u-chiu.

CH'ÊNG PO: Who was Kung-sun Ch'u-chiu?

CH'ÊNG YING: He and Chao Tun had both been at court together. Ch'êng Ying suggested that Kung-sun should report to the man in red that he, Ch'êng Ying, had hidden the orphan and let him kill them together, father and son. Then Kung-sun would be able to look after the orphan till he became of age to avenge his parents' death. Kung-sun Ch'u-chiu replied, 'I am already an old man. Since you are prepared to sacrifice your child by passing him off as the orphan, bring him here to me. You go and report to the man in red. Let me and your child die together. You hide the orphan, and later see he avenges his family. That will be the better plan.'

CH'ÊNG PO: This Ch'êng Ying, was he willing to sacrifice his own child?

CH'ÊNG YING: He was even willing to sacrifice his own life, not only that of his child. He took the baby, put him in Kung-sun's house, and went to report to the man in red. Kung-sun was tortured, the child was found and put to death, and Kung-sun committed suicide. Twenty years have passed since all this happened. The Orphan of Chao is now a man of twenty, and he has not yet avenged his parents. What more is there to say?

CH'ÊNG PO: Your story was such a long one, I feel as if I were asleep or in a dream. I simply don't understand.

CH'ÊNG YING: So you still don't understand. The man in red is really the villainous Tu-an Ku, Chao Tun was your grandfather, Chao Shuo the Emperor's son-in-law your father, the Princess Royal your mother!

CH'ÊNG PO: Then I am the Orphan of Chao! I don't know how I'll contain myself!

CH'ÊNG PO *faints;* CH'ÊNG YING *catches hold of him.*

CH'ÊNG YING: Young master, wake up!

CH'ÊNG PO: It's too painful to bear!

Would men of iron and stone not break out into a wail?
I will go to any length to take that villain alive.

CH'ÊNG YING: Today I have succeeded in bringing to full growth this offspring of the family of Chao. But my own family shall die with me! [*weeps*]

CH'ÊNG PO:

He and he alone it was put all our family to the sword:
I and I alone shall repay him with the lives of all his own.

CH'ÊNG YING: Say no more, young master, in case the evil Tu-an Ku should hear of this.

CH'ÊNG PO: Rest assured. Tomorrow I shall first see His Majesty and the rest of the court, and then I shall kill the villain myself.

Tomorrow when I meet with my enemy
I shall stop him straight where he stands.
I need no soldiers or attendants;
Using my strong arm only lightly
I shall drag him away like a dead dog,

Asking him only what has become of his conscience
And what of Heaven's sacred laws.
I shall take away his great seal of office,
Strip him of all his embroidered robes,
Bind his hands behind his back to the common stake,
And with a pincer pull out his spotted tongue,
With an awl pick out his villainous eyes,
With a fine dagger slit his body,
With an iron hammer break his bones,
Then with a bronze sword cut off his head. *Exeunt.*

ACT FIVE

Enter WEI CHIANG *followed by* CHANG CH'IEN.

WEI CHIANG: I am Wei Chiang, an official of the first rank. This morning Ch'êng Po petitioned His Majesty for leave to seize Tu-an Ku and avenge his father. I have His Majesty's orders to tell Ch'êng Po that Tu-an Ku still has the whole army under him and it is feared he might revolt; Ch'êng Po is advised to seize Tu-an Ku in secret and himself put his whole family to death. When this is done, additional titles and rewards will be his. I dare not let a word of this news leak out. I must deliver it myself. *Exeunt.*

Enter CH'ÊNG PO *leading his horse and holding a sword in his hand.*

CH'ÊNG PO:

Here in the market square the account can be settled,
No more than he shall I let him go lightly,
It will be like a tiger pouncing on a sheep.
I shall see what precautions the villain has taken,

I shall exact the vengeance that has gathered twenty years:
Life for life to repay three hundred deaths.
If I should die it is small matter.

Enter TU-AN KU *with* SOLDIERS.

TU-AN KU: I am going home from headquarters. Make a way for me and take your time.

CH'ÊNG PO: Isn't that the old villain coming?

See how proudly his bodyguard precede him row by row,
How noisily his attendants follow at his sides.
See how he puffs up his chest,
How he makes show of his power!
Here with my charger swift as a torrent,
The sword I draw as sharp as autumn frost,
I come forward to stop him in his way.

TU-AN KU: What brings you here, Ch'êng Po?

CH'ÊNG PO: You old villain! I am not Ch'êng Po. I am the Orphan of Chao. Twenty years ago you butchered more than three hundred members of my family. Today I am taking you in revenge for them.

TU-AN KU: Who told you this?

CH'ÊNG PO: Ch'êng Ying.

TU-AN KU: This bodes no good. I had better get out of here quickly.

CH'ÊNG PO: You villain, where are you going?

Already he is so frightened his soul is hovering in the air.
No, no, no! nothing can excuse him now.

CH'ÊNG PO *lays hold of* TU-AN KU *and* CH'ÊNG YING *hurries in.*

CH'ÊNG YING: I was afraid my young master might have come to some harm, and I have followed after him to see if I can help. Heaven be praised! my young master has taken Tu-an Ku.

CH'ÊNG PO: Someone bind this fellow and bring him to the Emperor. *Exeunt.*

Enter WEI CHIANG *and* CHANG CH'IEN.

WEI CHIANG: Go to the door. If anyone comes report to me.

Enter CH'ÊNG PO *and* CH'ÊNG YING *with* TU-AN KU, *bound.*

CH'ÊNG PO: Father, you and I are to go to see His Majesty. [*sees* WEI CHIANG] Sir, we have taken Tu-an Ku.

WEI CHIANG: Bring him here. You, Tu-an Ku, you murderer of the loyal and good, you treacherous villain, what have you to say?

TU-AN KU: If I had succeeded I would have become emperor; now I have failed I am no better than a captive slave. Since it has come to this, all I beg of you is a speedy death.

CH'ÊNG PO: You, sir, shall decide for me.

WEI CHIANG: You say you wish for a speedy death. I on the other hand wish your death to be a lingering one. Nail this villain to the Wooden Donkey, scrape him into shreds. And only when all his skin and flesh are gone, cut off his head and rip open his belly. Don't let him die too soon.

CH'ÊNG YING: Today you have your revenge, young master, and your name is at last restored to you. But on whom shall I, a lonely old man, depend?

CH'ÊNG PO:

> How many would sacrifice their own child for one of
> another name?

Such generosity and goodness are not easily forgotten.
I shall summon a painter of the highest rank
To make a memorial of your true likeness,
To be worshipped ever after in our family temple.

WEI CHIANG: Ch'êng Ying and Ch'êng Po, face the Palace and kneel, and hear the Emperor's decree: How true it is that the laws of Heaven reach far and wide. We congratulate ourself that the Orphan of Chao has been able to take his revenge and bring this treacherous official to his doom. The Orphan's name shall be restored to him: we bestow upon him the name of Chao Wu. He shall inherit all the titles and positions of his father and grandfather. The son of General Han Chüeh shall hold the rank of general; a thousand acres of land shall be given to Ch'êng Ying; for Kung-sun Ch'u-chiu a tomb shall be erected with a memorial in stone; and all those remaining who lost their lives in this cause shall be honoured by public proclamation. Henceforth, through the length and breadth of the kingdom, a new life shall begin. Let us all raise our heads in praise of the Emperor's infinite virtue.

THE SOUL OF CH'IEN-NÜ LEAVES HER BODY

by
Chêng Teh-hui
(*early fourteenth century*)

THE SOUL OF CH'IEN-NÜ LEAVES HER BODY

據明崇禎刻本柳枝集影印

CHARACTERS

MRS CHANG, *Ch'ien-nü's mother*
WANG WÊN-CHÜ, *betrothed to Ch'ien-nü*
CH'IEN-NÜ, *daughter to Mrs Chang*
MEI-HSIANG, *Ch'ien-nü's maid*
THE SOUL OF CH'IEN-NÜ
CHANG CH'IEN, *servant to Wang Wên-chü*

SERVANTS *and* ATTENDANTS

THE SOUL OF CH'IEN-NÜ LEAVES HER BODY

THE WEDGE

Enter MRS CHANG *with her* SERVANTS.

MRS CHANG: I am Mrs Chang. My husband died long ago. We had only one daughter, Ch'ien-nü, now seventeen years old. She sews and cooks and does everything well. When my husband was alive he had our daughter betrothed, as the custom was, to the unborn child of a certain Mr Wang. The child was born and was a boy, named Wên-chü. He is already grown up and I've been told he is very studious. Several times I have written to him, and the child replies that he will be coming soon to be married to Ch'ien-nü.

Enter WANG WÊN-CHÜ.

WANG WÊN-CHÜ: I am Wang Wên-chü. Both my parents, sad to say, are dead. My future mother-in-law has written to me on several occasions concerning my marriage to her daughter. Now that the time has come for the imperial examination, I am going to Chang-an to sit for it and to visit my future mother-in-law at the same time. Here is the place. Will someone go inside and say that Wang Wên-chü is at the gate?

SERVANT: Madam, there is a young student at the gate saying that he is Wang Wên-chü.

MRS CHANG: The words had hardly left my lips and my child has come. Ask him please to come in.

WANG WÊN-CHÜ *sees* MRS CHANG.

WANG WÊN-CHÜ: I am very sorry that my visit has been so long delayed. Please sit down, mother, and receive my respects.

WANG WÊN-CHÜ *kneels and kowtows.*

MRS CHANG: Please get up, child.
WANG WÊN-CHÜ: I have come to pay my respects first, then I am on my way to sit for the imperial examination.
MRS CHANG: Go and tell Mei-hsiang to ask her young mistress to come here and greet her elder brother.
SERVANT: Yes, madam.

Enter CH'IEN-NÜ *followed by* MEI-HSIANG.

CH'IEN-NÜ: I am Ch'ien-nü. Mother is calling for me. I don't know what it can be about. Follow me, Mei-hsiang. [*sees* MRS CHANG]
MRS CHANG: Pay your respects to your elder brother, child. [CH'IEN-NÜ *bows to* WANG WÊN-CHÜ.] My child, this is Ch'ien-nü. You may go back to your room now.

CH'IEN-NÜ *goes out of the room with* MEI-HSIANG.

CH'IEN-NÜ: But I have no elder brother, Mei-hsiang.
MEI-HSIANG: Don't you recognize him? Why, he is the one you were engaged to before he was born.
CH'IEN-NÜ: So he is the young man Wang. But my mother asked me to greet him as an elder brother. I can't think what she means by it.

Well suited in our talents, well matched in our looks,

My mother on the Road of Love
Has raised high a wall of Rain and Clouds,
Intending to separate a woman from her love,
The longing girl and lonely boy bringing sorrow on each other.
If you had not restrained me I may never have thought of him,
But the more you keep me from him
The more he will live in my heart. *Exeunt.*

MRS CHANG: Tidy the library so that my child can settle down to revise his studies. Don't forget to take him his tea and his meals.

WANG WÊN-CHÜ: Please don't trouble to tidy the library, mother. I shall be going straight to the capital to sit for the examination.

MRS CHANG: Stay for just a day or two, my child. It won't delay you. *Exeunt.*

ACT ONE

Enter CH'IEN-NÜ *followed by* MEI-HSIANG.

CH'IEN-NÜ: Since I met Wang Wên-chü I feel as if my soul were afloat and wandering away. Who could have thought that my mother would regret that Wang Wên-chü and I were engaged to be married? What does she intend to do? This autumn weather, how it makes one sad!

Suffering through the chilly night,
The sound of the wind startled and woke me.
Through the gauze window dawn is breaking,
The wind is rustling among falling leaves,
They cover all the ground, no one sweeps them away.

This is the true weather of late autumn!
All that lies within my heart is gathered at my brow.
I have not looked into the mirror,
The embroidery needle I have not touched,
Hating to sit at night before the window in the dim
  candle shadow,
Unable to bear being made up in my chamber with
  the moon on high.
My nature overflows with love, love for my future
  husband,
He is the very pattern of a man.
But many a moonlit night and flower-filled dawn we
  waste,
Destined not to meet,
But to partake of suffering and grief.
In love so silent how can I dispel my gloom?
I grow sick and fearful lest my mother should know.
To look afar,
The heavens are vast, the earth is small;
The deeper dyed,
My dreams are shattered and my soul is tired.

MEI-HSIANG: Do not distress yourself, young mistress.
CH'IEN-NÜ: When will it end, Mei-hsiang, this state of things?

If he has not taken to his bed,
I think he will be thinner now.
Though he has not yet travelled far,
Already my love is tracing distant clouds,
And my tears are falling like the sound of rain.
I cannot lean against the railing counting the curving
  lakes and mountains,

It is like looking to the ends of the world to descry
one small green hill.

He has sent me poems and he too is resentful of my mother.

It is the injustice that he mostly feels,
It is that which he expresses;
His heart's desires not yet fulfilled,
Of these he makes his poems.
Earnestly and wholly he offers his love,
Displays his elegance,
Makes boast of his talents.
I have studied carefully how he composes his lines,
And marked how he uses his brush;
I know he is a scholar of lofty ambitions.
But this sorrow, when will it end?
Each of us alone, with little fortune.
I prepare for the sleep of love
Amid perfumes of quilted brocade,
He awaits the songs of love
To the tunes of nuptial harmony.
Could we not be butterflies on the wing
Around a flowering tree?

MEI-HSIANG: The student is no ordinary young man, and with looks such as yours you two are perfectly matched.
CH'IEN-NÜ: What are we going to do, Mei-hsiang?

Each day for me is a year to endure,
Happy days are few.
Of the Thirty-three Heavens I see,
The highest is the Heaven of Parting Sorrow.
Of the Four Hundred and Four ailments to contract,
How is the sickness of Love to be endured?

Now he plans to sit for the examination.

A thousand leagues away you raise your hopes to
 mount the palace steps,
At one bound like a salmon leaping you are through
 the Dragon Gate,
There to be married to a second wife,
Wickedly beautiful though she may be.

MEI-HSIANG: Indeed in his looks and his talents he is equally fine.

CH'IEN-NÜ:

Surely he soars above the Yellow Dust,
And walks among the azure clouds.
He cannot be compared to the disturbers of the
 peaceful dawn,
The swallows and sparrows beneath the cottage eaves;
He is rather a leviathan
Whipping up storms and whirling seas.

MEI-HSIANG: He is going today.

CH'IEN-NÜ: Let us go to the Willow-Breaking Pavilion to see him off.[1] *Exeunt.*

Enter WANG WÊN-CHÜ *and* MRS CHANG *with* SERVANTS.

WANG WÊN-CHÜ: Today is a lucky and auspicious day. I must start my long journey to the capital.

MRS CHANG: Since you must go, I shall see you off at the Willow-Breaking Pavilion. Go and ask the young mistress to come.

Enter CH'IEN-NÜ *and* MEI-HSIANG.

CH'IEN-NÜ: Here I am, mother.

MRS CHANG: Come and say good-bye to your brother at the Willow-Breaking Pavilion, child. Bring a cup of wine.

CH'IEN-NÜ: Yes, mother. [CH'IEN-NÜ *pours wine and hands it to* WANG WÊN-CHÜ.] Drink this cup of wine, brother!

WANG WÊN-CHÜ *drinks.*

WANG WÊN-CHÜ: Now I am leaving, mother, there is something I must ask you. It concerns the marriage between Ch'ien-nü and myself. My parents are both dead. For years we have been unable to marry. When I first came I asked you about it, but you made Ch'ien-nü call me her elder brother. What does it mean? I dare not do what I myself think best. I know what you have planned can't be mistaken, mother.

MRS CHANG: What you say is right and proper, my child. It is for this reason I think you should address each other as brother and sister: For three generations now we have never married a daughter of the family to anyone who has not held an official position. Consider, you have finished your studies and are well-versed in the classics, but you haven't yet passed the imperial examination. Now you are going to the capital. Pass the examination, have yourself appointed to some official position, then come back and marry Ch'ien-nü. Isn't this the best thing to do?

WANG WÊN-CHÜ: If that is the case, mother, then I thank you. I must set out on my long journey.

CH'IEN-NÜ: When you are made an official, you must not marry another woman.

WANG WÊN-CHÜ: Set your mind at rest. As soon as I obtain an official appointment I shall come back and we shall be married.

CH'IEN-NÜ: How hard it is to say good-bye!

As Ch'u marshes are deep,
Ch'in passes distant,
Mount T'ai and Mount Hua high,
I sigh, for life –
So many partings, meetings how few!

WANG WÊN-CHÜ: When I become an official you'll become a lady of high position.

CH'IEN-NÜ:

The wine in the cup
I drink with tears,
What is in my heart
Let me speak to you.
Like the tender willow branch I break and offer you here,
Do not let your love bear leaves without the deeper root.
Now I must live emptily through unhappy nights!
Oh how is this sorrow to end!

WANG WÊN-CHÜ: I have been thinking of you constantly too.

CH'IEN-NÜ: That is the more distressing now.

The bamboos outside the window rustle their emerald tops,
The grass lies deep below the mossy steps.
The study is suddenly deserted,
The house silent; nobody comes.
How are my sorrows to be dispelled!
Now is the most unbearable time.
Tonight where will you moor your boat?

The sail will not be furled
In the cruel west wind.
Like curling snow the waves will swell,
The shadows of the bank rise high,
For a thousand leagues river and clouds float by.
Don't be like wild swan shedding no feather for news.
It is an old saying,
'All good things soon come to an end.'
If you must go, don't take your heart also.

MRS CHANG: Fetch the carriage, Mei-hsiang, and accompany the young mistress home.

MEI-HSIANG: Will you get into the carriage, young mistress?

WANG WÊN-CHÜ: Please, now, go back. I must be on my way.

CH'IEN-NÜ:

Here my green-curtained carriage I delay,
There he hesitates to mount his golden stirrups;
My silken sleeves are wet with tears,
His whip lets hang its green jade tip.
Ahead are sorrows heaped high where the west wind blows on the ancient road,
And a heart full of care for him I love is gone.
If Heaven so deep and blue could love, Heaven too would grow old.

WANG WÊN-CHÜ: Be assured. As soon as I obtain an official appointment I shall come back to marry you. Get into the carriage, I beg you, and go home.

CH'IEN-NÜ:

From now on,
Mine only to write of sorrow on the plantain leaves,

No need to interpret dreams, consult the fortune-
telling sticks.
What mind have I
To change my ornaments of pearl, my necklace of
green jade?
Now he has gone
My true loving soul takes wing;
It will not leave him, on all sides it will surround him.
I know that long before he returns with fame and
honour
He will have broken his vow of love. *Exeunt.*

ACT TWO

Enter MRS CHANG, *worried.*

MRS CHANG: After Ch'ien-nü had seen Wang Wên-chü off at the Willow-Breaking Pavilion and returned home, she fell ill and took to her bed, and she hasn't been able to leave it since. I have called doctors to see her but she is no better; in fact her illness is growing more and more serious. What's to be done? I will go and see if she needs anything. *Exit.*

Enter WANG WÊN-CHÜ.

WANG WÊN-CHÜ: I have been thinking of Ch'ien-nü constantly since we parted, and I cannot rest for worrying. Our boat is moored by the riverbank. With my *ch'in* on my lap I will play some music to console myself.

WANG WÊN-CHÜ *plays the* ch'in. *Enter* THE SOUL OF CH'IEN-NÜ.

THE SOUL OF CH'IEN-NÜ: Since I said good-bye to Wang Wên-chü I can no longer merely think of him. Far better to follow him and go with him. Without telling my mother I have hastened straight after him. Wang Wên-chü, you thought nothing of leaving me. You cannot know how I have passed the time!

> If I do not reach him while he moors by the riverbank,
> When will he return on horseback to our gate?
> Silently and faintly,
> Loftily and daintily,
> I tread the sandy banks,
> Walking in bright moonlight;
> I have seen a thousand mountains and ten thousand streams
> All in the twinkling of an eye.
> Heart unable to forget our parting sorrow,
> I hasten to reach his boat beyond the willows,
> Sweat in many pearls on my shining face,
> Hair swept up in ravens' wings a dishevelled cloud about my head.
> I am exhausted with walking.
> Is it at a tavern on some Ch'in Huai river you have moored the night?

How long my walk has been! Here is the river's edge. I hear people talking and shouting. Let me see.

> Suddenly I hear horses neighing and the sound of voices,
> Though indistinct beneath the weeping willows.
> A sudden fright sets my heart trembling –
> It is someone fishing, beating a board.
> I will listen here quietly to what the west wind brings.
> The grass at the sand's edge is slippery with frost,

My green gauze skirt swept wet,
With dews more drenched than ever on mossy steps
my shoes.
See the river at twilight, how like a painting it is –
An ice jar brimful of water, with Heaven above and
below;
A jade of flawless green.
Look, the distant bank, the lone wild duck, the
evening hues,
Dry vines, old trees, ravens in the dusk.
Listen, the long note of a flute – from where does it
come?
And the sound of a song sung to the creak of an oar.

The sound of a *ch'in* on the prow of a boat! Could it be Wang Wên-chü? Let me listen.

WANG WÊN-CHÜ: The night is far gone. I hear a woman's voice on the bank. It sounds like that of my Ch'ien-nü. Ch'ien-nü, is that you? When did you come here, and why?

THE SOUL OF CH'IEN-NÜ [*sees* WANG WÊN-CHÜ]: Wang Wên-chü, so it is you! Mother doesn't know but I have left and come straight to be with you. Let us go together to the capital.

WANG WÊN-CHÜ: How did you come, by carriage or on horse?

THE SOUL OF CH'IEN-NÜ:

I am almost exhausted with walking.
Unhappy me! I pined for you,
Heart yearning,
When to cease?
You left me.
When next you see me,

If I have not wasted away
Most likely I shall be at death's door.

WANG WÊN-CHÜ: If your mother comes to hear of this, what's to be done?

THE SOUL OF CH'IEN-NÜ:

If she should overtake me,
What can she do?
The common saying has it,
'Be bold in all you do.'

WANG WÊN-CHÜ [*angrily*]: There's an ancient proverb which says 'Marry and you're a wife; elope, and you're a concubine.' Your mother has promised that we shall be married. Why not wait until I've obtained an official position and return? Let our two families be united then. Won't all then be perfect in the eyes of the world? Now you have come alone and in secret. This is against all custom and a breach of your duty. What reason have you?

THE SOUL OF CH'IEN-NÜ:

Now your colour rises and you fly into a rage.
My heart is set on not returning home.
It is only out of love I come,
Not to intimidate you.
I am resolved – no more dilemma.

WANG WÊN-CHÜ: Go back quickly, Ch'ien-nü.

THE SOUL OF CH'IEN-NÜ:

I thought you only in a hurry to go on your journey,
But you are worried and anxious, playing your *ch'in.*
And am I not unhappy too, and my *p'i pa* wet with
tears?

What do I care to make my dishevelled hair sleek at
  my temples as cicada's wings,
To draw my eyebrows lightly black.
Like falling catkins and flying flowers,
Who would question if the traveller fares better than
  the stay-at-home?
More than this what can I say –
I long for the autumn wind to steer the tall sail.

I have come after you for one reason only: I must make sure of you.

WANG WÊN-CHÜ: What must you make sure of?

THE SOUL OF CH'IEN-NÜ:

When you come from the Royal Graduates' Feast in
  the Garden of Jade Wood,
Matchmakers will stop your horse,
Lifting and praising portraits of beautiful women,
Claiming they were born in the family of prime
  ministers, dukes or kings.
And enthralled with a life of luxury,
You may marry happily into one of these families.

WANG WÊN-CHÜ: I am going on this journey only to take part in the examination. If I succeed, how can I forget you?

THE SOUL OF CH'IEN-NÜ: If you pass the examination . . .

WANG WÊN-CHÜ: If I don't pass the examination, what then?

THE SOUL OF CH'IEN-NÜ: If you don't, then a wooden hairpin and a plain cotton skirt for me. I am willing to live with you for better or worse.

WANG WÊN-CHÜ: Since you are so loyal and determined, come with me to the capital.

THE SOUL OF CH'IEN-NÜ: You will take me with you!

Call the captain, quick!
I am afraid my family should catch me up.
First hoist high the cloud-soaring sail,
Into the bright moon keep a straight course.
Even if the east wind should blow,
Don't delay.
Quick, let us be on our way! *Exeunt.*

ACT THREE

Enter WANG WÊN-CHÜ *and* ATTENDANTS.

WANG WÊN-CHÜ: Bring me a brush and ink. [*writes*] 'Since I came to the capital, I have taken the imperial examination and passed first with the highest honours. Once I have been awarded an official position, I shall return home with the young mistress.' Call Chang Ch'ien.

Enter CHANG CH'IEN.

CHANG CH'IEN:

I'm a pretty good servant as servants go,
Here and there on official chores.
I walk three hundred miles in a day,
It's only the next I can stop for a pause.

What can I do for you, Your Honour?

WANG WÊN-CHÜ: Take this letter, a family letter with good news, and go straight to Hêng-chou and deliver it at the house of Chang Kung-pi. And when you see Mrs Chang, tell her that I have been made an official. *Exeunt.*

Enter MRS CHANG.

MRS CHANG: Ch'ien-nü is ill in bed. She talks and laughs. I

don't know what she is suffering from. It is two days since I saw her. I must go and see her now. *Exit.*

Enter CH'IEN-NÜ, *ill, supported by* MEI-HSIANG.

CH'IEN-NÜ: Since Wang Wên-chü took his leave of me, I've been stricken with this illness. Whenever I close my eyes I am with him at once. This lovesickness is killing me.

Since we clasped hands and said farewell,
I am left languishing, and all in vain.
Surely the bitterest thing in life is parting.
When I speak I have little strength,
When I lie down I cannot sleep;
Of food and drink I cannot tell the taste,
No use the medicines I take,
There is no cure.
I know this secret sickness,
When it began.
If I am to be well again,
It will not be till I see him.
One moment I am floating,
Bereft of my soul,
The next all is clear,
And I am myself –
Then all is confusion again,
And I cannot tell Heaven from Earth.

I see only Wang Wên-chü before me. But was it you, Mei-hsiang? What time of the year is it?

MEI-HSIANG: The spring is almost over. The leaves are darkening and the blossoms are fewer now. It is nearly April.

CH'IEN-NÜ:

The days grow long, and longer my sorrows;
The blossoms grow scarce, and scarcer his letters.

Wang Wên-chü, so you can endure it all!

Suddenly spring has come and gone and you have not returned.

MEI-HSIANG: It is not a year yet since he went away, why do you think of him like this?

CH'IEN-NÜ:

Though I say we are parted scores of years,
Though separated ten thousand miles,
To count the days till his return
I have made marks in the bamboo grove on every emerald stalk.
When he went away,
It was the time of willows, west winds, autumn days.
Now the time of pear flowers, evening rain, the Han Shih Festival has passed again.

MEI-HSIANG: Have you not consulted the fortune-tellers?

CH'IEN-NÜ:

The tortoise-shell divination is unsure,[2]
It is vain to beg signs,
Spiders are untrustworthy,
Magpies lie.
The candle-wax petals, what do they tell of happiness?

Enter MRS CHANG.

MRS CHANG: Is the young mistress better, Mei-hsiang?

CH'IEN-NÜ: Who is that?

MEI-HSIANG: Your mother has come to see you.

CH'IEN-NÜ: Day after day I see only Wang Wên-chü. I don't see my mother coming.

MRS CHANG: How are you, my child?

CH'IEN-NÜ:

Love is the most fatal sickness of all,
Like yesternight's drunkenness in the spell of spring sleep,
Like bright snowy catkins whirling over the paths of the meadow,
Like swallows riding on the east wind west of the pavilion.
I am young and I am cast away,
Ungrateful to my youth and fair weather.
In the sadness of separation my longing has grown,
I find no delight even in Nature's display.
The chirp of a bird will startle my sorrowful heart.
Let my unhappy life end while spring is here,
And my soul chase an expanse of flying flowers.

CH'IEN-NÜ *faints.*

MRS CHANG: Wake up, child!

CH'IEN-NÜ *comes to herself.*

CH'IEN-NÜ:

Already ill
And there comes a new sickness,
This fainting –
It is nothing but Death hurrying close,
No medicine can reach this disease.

MRS CHANG: I'll send for another doctor, one of the best.

CH'IEN-NÜ:

And if he comes,
How can he be better than the best of doctors?

MRS CHANG: I'll send someone to ask Wang Wên-chü to come back.

CH'IEN-NÜ:

Send for him!
Why when you first invited him
Did you not make him your son-in-law?
Now it is too late for regret.

MRS CHANG: He has gone and there's no news from him.

CH'IEN-NÜ:

And why is there no news from him?
There are two reasons
I already know.
Having been made an official he has married another,
Or having failed his examination he is ashamed to return home.

MRS CHANG: You are not to distress yourself so, child. For the time being you must rest and get yourself well.

CH'IEN-NÜ:

You see I endure a thousand deaths, a thousand ends,
Struck down half human, half a ghost.

I feel drowsy. Let me sleep.

Exeunt MRS CHANG *and* MEI-HSIANG.

Enter WANG WÊN-CHÜ; *sees* CH'IEN-NÜ.

WANG WÊN-CHÜ: I have come to see you, Ch'ien-nü.

CH'IEN-NÜ: Where have you come from, Wang Wên-chü?
WANG WÊN-CHÜ: I have been made an official, Ch'ien-nü.
CH'IEN-NÜ:

I was saying you were ungrateful and faithless,
And you have passed the examination and been made an official.
Compared with the day we parted,
How much more splendid you are.

WANG WÊN-CHÜ: I must go, Ch'ien-nü. *Exit.*

CH'IEN-NÜ *awakes.*

CH'IEN-NÜ: I saw Wang Wên-chü plainly and he told me he had been made an official. But when I awoke it was all a dream.

He told me the truth,
Then hastened away.
I leapt up at once,
Already he was nowhere to be found.

Enter MEI-HSIANG.

MEI-HSIANG: Why this shouting?
CH'IEN-NÜ: I just dreamt that I saw Wang Wên-chü and he told me that he was now an official.

Enter CHANG CH'IEN.

CHANG CH'IEN: They told me this is the place. [CHANG CH'IEN *sees* MEI-HSIANG.] Excuse me.
MEI-HSIANG: Who are you?
CHANG CH'IEN: Is this the house of the Chang family?
MEI-HSIANG: Yes, it is. Why do you ask?

CHANG CH'IEN: I come from the capital. My master Wang Wên-chü is now an official. He has sent me with a letter for Mrs Chang.

MEI-HSIANG: Wait here. I'll tell the young mistress. [MEI-HSIANG *approaches* CH'IEN-NÜ.] Wang Wên-chü has been appointed an official. He has sent someone with a letter. He's at the gate.

CH'IEN-NÜ: Ask him to come here.

MEI-HSIANG: You, with the letter. You may go in and see the young mistress.

CHANG CH'IEN *sees* CH'IEN-NÜ *and is taken aback.*

CHANG CH'IEN [*aside*]: What a splendid woman! She is just like the mistress of the house at home. [*aloud*] I've been sent by my master Wang Wên-chü with a letter to Mrs Chang.

CH'IEN-NÜ: Hand me the letter, Mei-hsiang.

MEI-HSIANG: Hand over the letter, you.

CHANG CH'IEN *hands over the letter;* CH'IEN-NÜ *reads.*

CH'IEN-NÜ: 'Since I came to the capital, I have taken the imperial examination and passed first with the highest honours. Once I have been awarded an official position, I shall return home with the young mistress.' So he has a wife now! I am so angry I could die!

CH'IEN-NÜ *faints;* MEI-HSIANG *goes to her.*

MEI-HSIANG: Wake up, young mistress, wake up! [CH'IEN-NÜ *comes to.*] This is all your fault, you with your letter!

MEI-HSIANG *beats* CHANG CH'IEN.

CH'IEN-NÜ: Wang Wên-chü, you have broken my heart.

To think over all the past again –
A love to last a hundred years

Is brought to nothing but a heavy sigh.
Think of past days, the study beside the bamboo grove,
The pavilion beyond the willows where we parted,
How we lingered!
Now comes the drizzle, dark clouds start to gather.
From now on
Lonely hours,
Unhappy days,
Attended at my pillow by the demon Sickness.
For a whole spring there came no news;
Now the long-awaited letter arrives.
I imagined the faithful ink would fill the page with
thoughts of love;
In fact it is a divorce note in an envelope more.
I am so angry not all my tears could ease my pain.
I have borne everything until today.
Is this my reward for caring nothing for death,
for throwing my life away?

Exeunt CH'IEN-NÜ *and* MEI-HSIANG.

CHANG CH'IEN: It's all my master's fault. If you've married, well and good, but why do you send me to deliver this letter? I thought you said it was a family letter with good news. In fact it's nothing but a divorce note. It upset the young mistress so much she fainted, and Mei-hsiang gave me a beating. It's all my master's fault.

I don't think he can know what he's doing,
This letter he sent caused nothing but gloom.
If he sends me to deliver a letter again,
I'll be like a tortoise – keep my head tucked well in. *Exit.*

ACT FOUR

Enter WANG WÊN-CHÜ *with* ATTENDANTS.

WANG WÊN-CHÜ:

No joys ever came like present joys,
No happiness ever happier than today's.

I have been here in the capital with my wife for three years. Thanks to His Majesty I have been made prefect of Hêng-chou. Make ready, attendants. I am going to take up the position today.

Enter THE SOUL OF CH'IEN-NÜ.

THE SOUL OF CH'IEN-NÜ: At last the day has come. You and I, in the embroidered gowns of an official and his wife, are going home.

For months, for years, we tarried in the capital,
Hearing only across the garden the cuckoo's song
Urging us to start our journey home.
When over all the past
I cast my mind,
I feel as if I were not yet quite awake
And dream a dream of neglecting duty and forsaking home.
But think of my love's disposition,
Has he not bought wisdom from the Lord of Heaven,
And do his inward talents not match his outward grace?
To see him one cannot but be moved to love him,
So true and so sincere
He could make one throw one's life away
And lose one's soul to him.

WANG WÊN-CHÜ: Let the horse go slowly.

THE SOUL OF CH'IEN-NÜ:

> I am riding a steed,
> A quick and eager young beast,
> That carries me like a piece of paper unmanageably light.
> It rears, I cannot hold it by pulling at the reins.
> It leaps like fire, I can scarcely keep in the saddle.
> We have ridden this long journey of ten stations or more not once pasturing.
> How thin it is, how light its hoofs!
> Scenes of late spring rouse my emotions;
> I blame the road full of blossoming flowers,
> Cluster after cluster of green willows, red apricots,
> Pair upon pair of purple swallows, yellow orioles,
> Two by two the bees, the butterflies.
> Each accompanies the other.
> I believe the Lord of Heaven knows how they live,
> And would have them set an example to mankind.

Enter MRS CHANG.

WANG WÊN-CHÜ: We have reached home already. Let me go in first. [WANG WÊN-CHÜ *sees* MRS CHANG *and kneels before her.*] I hope you will forgive me for what I have done.

MRS CHANG: What is there to be forgiven?

WANG WÊN-CHÜ: I ought not to have taken Ch'ien-nü with me to the capital without telling you.

MRS CHANG: Ch'ien-nü has fallen ill and still lies sick in her bed. She has not left the house. Where did you say Ch'ien-nü was?

THE SOUL OF CH'IEN-NÜ *appears.*

This must be a demon!

THE SOUL OF CH'IEN-NÜ:

Have pity on me, all alone, alone,
I cannot hold back the tears that fill my eyes.
Let me beat my breast, let me confess.
I sighed,
Grew sad,
Was filled with regret;
I followed my own will.
My mother is known to be shrewish;
Lacking all feeling between mother and child.

WANG WÊN-CHÜ: You little demon! What devilish spirit are you? Tell me the truth, or I'll cut you in two with this sword.

WANG WÊN-CHÜ *draws his sword ready to strike;*
THE SOUL OF CH'IEN-NÜ *takes fright.*

THE SOUL OF CH'IEN-NÜ: How is this all to end!

Why for no reason do you thunder and roar?
Suddenly you gave me such a fright.
This is all the fault of my mother,
Hoping to save the family's good name.
She pretends to be stupefied.
Demon! what demon?
For the sake of our past love
Let me go,
And let my mother see for herself who I am.

MRS CHANG: Don't let her go, Wang Wên-chü. She says she is not a demon spirit. Send her to the room and let her say which of the two women there is her servant Mei-hsiang.

Enter MEI-HSIANG *supporting* CH'IEN-NÜ *in a swoon;* THE SOUL OF CH'IEN-NÜ *sees* CH'IEN-NÜ.

THE SOUL OF CH'IEN-NÜ:

I cannot stand firmly,
I cannot walk steadily,
I see ornaments and cosmetics,
My head reels,
My heart trembles.
I see a group of young maids,
Incessantly talking,
Incessantly gesturing,
Supporting a beautiful woman almost half dead,
Who will not waken to their calls,
Who will not answer to their cries.
Now let me return to my body and be one.

THE SOUL OF CH'IEN-NÜ *passes into* CH'IEN-NÜ'*s body.*

MEI-HSIANG: Young mistress, young mistress, Wang Wên-chü has come back.

CH'IEN-NÜ [*awakes*]: Where is Wang Wên-chü?

WANG WÊN-CHÜ: Where is Ch'ien-nü?

MEI-HSIANG: When the other young mistress passed into the body of our young mistress, she woke up.

CH'IEN-NÜ *sees* WANG WÊN-CHÜ.

WANG WÊN-CHÜ: When I was made an official I sent Chang Ch'ien with a letter.

CH'IEN-NÜ:

Ah, you faithless and ungrateful man!
Today your heart's desires are satisfied.
When at last the long-awaited letter came,

It only served to puzzle me.
We heard you had passed the examination and become an official,
And were married to another; what was the meaning of this?
Should you ask me what has become of that woman,
Like a piece of paper I have torn her to shreds.

WANG WÊN-CHÜ: But you were with me in the capital for three years beyond a doubt. How is it that together you have become one person today?

CH'IEN-NÜ:

Remember that day when oars were raised and farewell cups drunk,
I feared the distant journey would weary our feverish dreams.
Suddenly my soul began to follow you in secret,
My body gave birth to another like my own,
Two fair-featured women each the image of the other.
One went with you to take the examination,
The other drowned in burning oil and withered in a sickness.
Mother, this was the soul of Ch'ien-nü leaving her body.

MRS CHANG: Such strange things happen in this world of ours! Today is an auspicious day and I shall see that the two of you are properly married. Kill a sheep and bring out the wine. We shall prepare a magnificent wedding feast!

THE INJUSTICE DONE TO TOU NGO

by

Kuan Han-ch'ing

(*1241?–1322?*)

THE INJUSTICE DONE TO TOU NGO

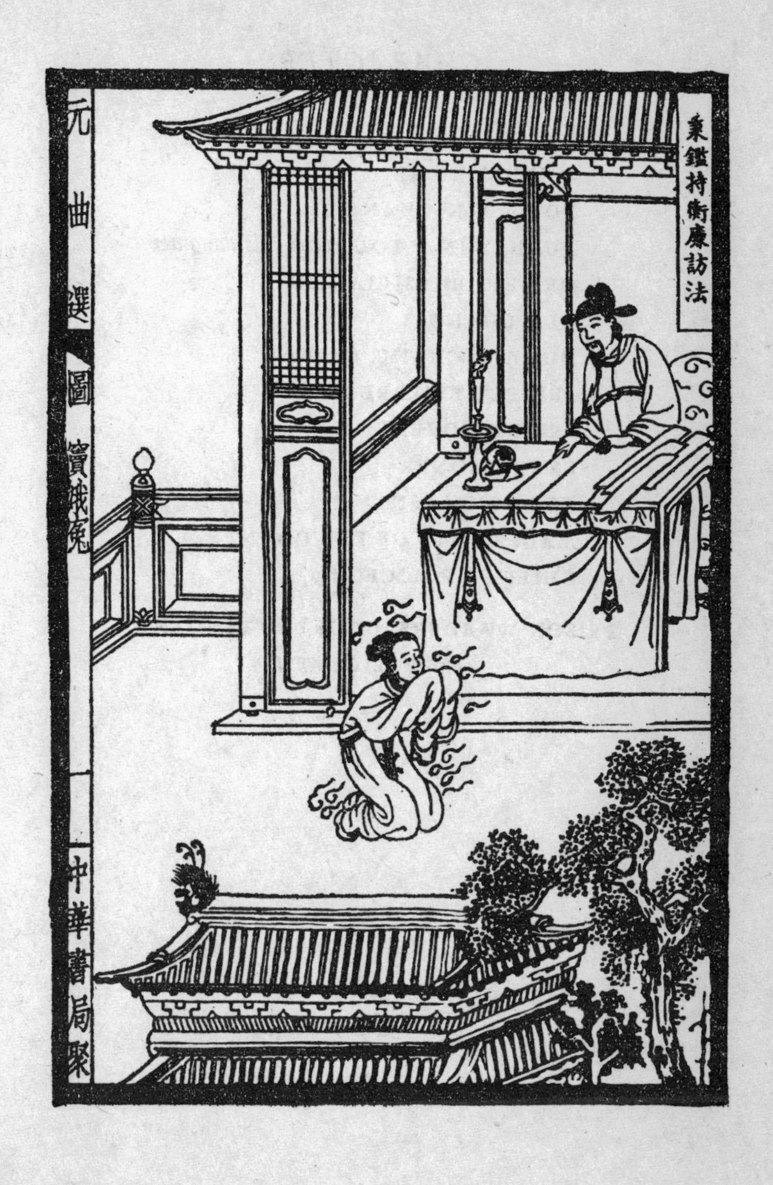

CHARACTERS

MOTHER TS'AI
TOU T'IEN-CHANG
TUAN-YÜN *or* TOU NGO, *his daughter*
DR BEST PHYSICIAN LU
OLD CHANG
DONKEY CHANG, *his son*
PREFECT EVILBRUTE
PRISON GOVERNOR
EXECUTIONER
CHANG CH'IEN
MAGISTRATE OF THE COUNTY
CHIEF OF POLICE

PRISON WARDERS, COURT ATTENDANTS
and POLICEMEN

THE INJUSTICE DONE TO TOU NGO

THE WEDGE

Enter MOTHER TS'AI.

MOTHER TS'AI:

> Flowers will bloom again another day,
> Man has never his youth again.
> No need for riches and honour always,
> We shall be gods if at peace and content.

I am old Mother Ts'ai. We were a family of three until my husband unfortunately died. We had one son only, now eight years of age. Our family is quite well-to-do. There is a scholar here named Tou. He borrowed twenty taels of silver from me last year, and now with the interest it ought to amount to forty taels. I have asked him for it several times but he keeps saying he is poor and hard up, and can't pay the debt. He has a daughter, seven this year, an agreeable child and lovely to look at. I've taken a fancy to her and wish to make her my daughter-in-law. I am prepared to cancel that debt of forty taels. We shall both benefit from it. He said that today was an auspicious day and that he would bring his daughter to me himself. He will be here any minute now.

Enter TOU T'IEN-CHANG *leading* TUAN-YÜN.

TOU T'IEN-CHANG: I am Tou T'ien-chang. From my childhood I was trained to be a Confucian scholar and I have studied a great deal. However fortune does not smile on me and I have failed to pass the imperial examination. Unfortunately my wife died, and left me with this daughter, Tuan-yün. Her mother died when she was three, and now she is seven years old. I am as poor as can be and have no choice but to settle down here in the city of Chu-chou. There is a certain Mother Ts'ai here who is very well-off. I've borrowed twenty taels of silver from her. I should have returned it to her by now with interest. She has asked for it several times, but how am I going to pay her? On a number of occasions Mother Ts'ai has asked people to come and say she would like to have my daughter for her daughter-in-law. Now the spring examinations are at hand and I am waiting to go to the capital to sit for them, but again I find myself in difficulties because I have no money to travel. Out of desperation I am sending my daughter to Mother Ts'ai to become her daughter-in-law. [*sighs*] Hm! Daughter-in-law? It is plainly nothing but selling her to Mother Ts'ai. This will cancel the forty taels of silver I owe her and besides this she will probably make me a small gift of money. If it's enough for me to go to sit for the examination it will be more than I can hope. Here I am talking and I've already arrived at her door. Is Mother Ts'ai at home?

MOTHER TS'AI: Please step inside, master scholar. I've been waiting for you for a long time.

TOU T'IEN-CHANG: I've come straight from home to bring my daughter to you. I won't presume to say that she is to be your daughter-in-law, I'd rather say she has come to run errands for you. Soon I shall be setting out for the capital for the imperial examination. I leave my daughter here and hope you will look after her.

MOTHER TS'AI: What are you saying? You are a member of

my family now. You owe me, with capital and interest, the sum of forty taels of silver in all. Here is the agreement; I return it to you. In addition I shall make you a gift of ten taels for your travelling expenses. It isn't much, I'm afraid.

TOU T'IEN-CHANG: How can I thank you, Mother Ts'ai! To begin with I owe you a large sum of money which you don't ask me to pay back; now you make me a gift for my travelling expenses. One day I shall repay this kindness many times over. If at any time you find my daughter foolish, for my sake be kind to her. She is only a child yet.

MOTHER TS'AI: You've no need to say. Now your daughter has come to my house I shall treat her as if she were my own. There'll be no need for you to worry at all.

TOU T'IEN-CHANG: When my child Tuan-yün deserves a beating, for my sake only scold her a little; when she deserves a scolding, say only a word or two. My child, things won't be the same now as when you were with me. I am your father and I overlook all your faults. But now you are here, and whenever you are naughty you are asking to be scolded and caned. There is nothing else I can do, my child. *Exit.*

TUAN-YÜN: Are you leaving your daughter behind, father? [*weeps*]

MOTHER TS'AI: You are now in my home. I am your mother-in-law and you are my very own daughter-in-law. You must think of us as your own flesh and blood. Don't cry! Come with me and you can help me about the house. *Exeunt.*

ACT ONE

Enter DR BEST PHYSICIAN LU.

DR LU:

In medicine there's room to change one's mind,
For prescriptions there's always the standard text;
There's no way of bringing the dead to life,
The living can always be doctored to death.

I am Dr Lu. They all say what a wonderful doctor I am! They call me Best Physician Lu. I have a chemist's shop at the South Gate of the city here in Shan-yang. There is a certain Mother Ts'ai in this city, and I have borrowed ten taels of silver from her. What with the interest, I have to pay her back twenty. Several times she's been here for the money, but I haven't got anything to pay her with. If she doesn't come again, everything'll be fine; if she does, I've got an idea. For the present I shall sit in my shop and wait to see if anyone comes.

Enter MOTHER TS'AI.

MOTHER TS'AI: Thirteen years ago the scholar Tou T'ien-chang left his child Tuan-yün with me to be my daughter-in-law. I changed her name, and called her Tou Ngo. Hardly two years had gone by after their marriage when my son died. My daughter-in-law still observes her widowhood. But three years have already passed, and soon she will no longer need to wear her widow's weeds. I told my daughter-in-law that I was going outside the city to Best Physician Lu to collect a debt. Here I am at his door. Is Best Physician Lu at home?

DR LU: At home, Mother Ts'ai.

MOTHER TS'AI: My money, I've waited a long time for it. Give it back to me and be done with it.

DR LU: I've no money at home, Mother Ts'ai. If you come with me to my farm I can pay you.

MOTHER TS'AI: Very well, lead the way.

DR LU *and* MOTHER TS'AI *walk about.*

DR LU [*aside*]: Here we are. There's no one anywhere about. Why not do it here, what's the point of waiting? I've a piece of rope with me. [*aloud*] Who's that calling you, Mother Ts'ai?

MOTHER TS'AI: Where?

DR LU *tries to strangle her;* OLD CHANG *and* DONKEY CHANG *rush in;* DR LU *takes to his heels in fright;* OLD CHANG *loosens the rope.*

DONKEY CHANG: This old woman was nearly strangled to death, father.

OLD CHANG: Where are you from, old lady, and what's your name? Why was that man trying to strangle you?

MOTHER TS'AI: I am Mother Ts'ai, and I'm a native of this city. I live alone at home with my widowed daughter-in-law. Dr Lu owes me twenty taels of silver and I went to get it back from him today. He lured me out to this lonely place and suddenly tried to strangle me. If it hadn't been for you, sir, and you, young gentleman, I wouldn't be alive now.

DONKEY CHANG: Did you hear what she says, father? She has a daughter-in-law at home. We've saved her life. She owes us something for that. Wouldn't it be a perfect arrangement if you had the old woman and I had the daughter-in-law? Wouldn't that suit both parties perfectly? You have a word with her.

OLD CHANG: Look here, old lady. You've no husband and I've no wife. How would you like to be married to me? What do you say?

MOTHER TS'AI: What's that you say! When I return home, I'll give you a large sum of money for my thanks.

DONKEY CHANG: Does that mean you're not willing? You only mentioned money on purpose to get round us. Dr Lu's rope is still here, I think I'll go on with the strangling.

DONKEY CHANG *takes up the rope.*

MOTHER TS'AI: Young gentleman, wait! Give me time to think about it.

DONKEY CHANG: What's there to think about? You have my father and I'll have your daughter-in-law.

MOTHER TS'AI [*aside*]: If I don't do what he says, he'll strangle me. Very well, very well! Come home with me, both of you. *Exeunt.*

Enter TOU NGO.

TOU NGO: I am Tou Ngo. When I was three my mother died; when I was seven my father left me. At seventeen I married my husband, and it is three years now since he died.

I am laden with misery,
For years I have endured.
Does Heaven know?
If Heaven knew my reasons,
I fear Heaven would be as haggard.

When will this misery end?

Is it my fate to be burdened my whole life with sorrow?
For whom but me is there no end to be seen?
The human heart is not like water ever to flow.

Is it because in my last life I burnt broken incense
sticks
That now I incur misfortune in this?
Make early preparations for your coming lives, I beg
you all.
I shall look after my mother-in-law,
I shall keep my widow's weeds.
Nothing shall make me break my vow.

My mother has gone to claim a debt. Why isn't she back yet?

Enter MOTHER TS'AI *with* OLD CHANG *and* DONKEY CHANG.

MOTHER TS'AI: Wait at the gate, both of you. Let me go in first.

DONKEY CHANG: You go in first, mother, and say that a son-in-law is at the gate.

MOTHER TS'AI *sees* TOU NGO.

TOU NGO: You've come back, mother. Have you had something to eat?

MOTHER TS'AI [*weeps*]: How am I going to say this, child? I feel so ashamed.

TOU NGO: Why are you crying, mother? Why are you so upset?

MOTHER TS'AI: I went to Dr Lu for the money. He took me out to some lonely place and there he tried to strangle me. Luckily a certain Mr Chang and his son Donkey Chang saved my life. And now Mr Chang wants to make me his wife. That's what's making me so upset.

TOU NGO: This won't do, mother. Give yourself time to think it over. We have food to eat, clothes to wear, we aren't pressed for any debts. What is more, you're getting on in years now – you're over sixty. How could you be looking for a husband again?

MOTHER TS'AI: What you've said is all true, my child. But it was this man and his son who saved my life. I've already said that when I returned home I would give them a large sum of money and other things to show my gratitude. I don't know how, but they found out I had a daughter-in-law at home. They said that since we had no husbands and they had no wives, surely it was the will of Heaven that we should be married. If I didn't agree to what they suggested they threatened to strangle me on the spot just as Dr Lu would have done. I was nearly out of my wits with fright so not only did I promise to marry the old man myself but promised that you would marry his son. There was nothing else I could do, child.

TOU NGO:

> Old love at a single stroke despatched,
> The new couple in complete accord!
> Won't this make people laugh us to scorn?

MOTHER TS'AI: It was this man and his son who saved my life. As things are, I shouldn't mind people laughing at me.

TOU NGO:

> Think how from the first your husband provided for
> you,
> Planned for you,
> Bought lands and estates
> To feed you
> And clothe you,
> Expecting that when alone,

With none to depend on,
You and your son should have enough for your old age.
Father-in-law, you have laboured in vain!

MOTHER TS'AI: He's only waiting to be married, child, full of joy at the happy event. How am I going to answer him?

TOU NGO:

You say he is full of joy,
But I fear endless shame will be yours,
Shame that you cannot bring yourself to swallow the nuptial wine,
Shame that with your poor eyesight you cannot fasten the One-Heart button.

MOTHER TS'AI: Stop railing at me, child. The old man and his son are waiting at the gate. Since things have come to this pass, you might as well take a husband.

TOU NGO: If you want a husband, you go ahead, mother. I certainly have no wish for one.

MOTHER TS'AI: Who said anything about wanting a husband? The two of them arrived without asking! What am I going to do?

DONKEY CHANG: We're to be married into the family today!

With shining bright hats
We are bridegrooms today,
Sleeves narrow and smart,
We are bridegrooms today.
What bridegrooms! What bridegrooms!
Just the right sort! Just the right sort!

OLD CHANG *and* DONKEY CHANG *come forward bowing.*

TOU NGO: You scoundrels, stand back! [*aside*]

> I fear my mother-in-law has no desire to keep her vow.
> Today she has found herself a vulgar old man
> With another in tow, some scapegrace of a fellow.

DONKEY CHANG [*making faces*]: Look at the pair of us! What physiques! Where will you find any husbands to compare! Don't miss this wonderful opportunity! [*to* TOU NGO] You and I kneel down and kowtow to Heaven and Earth, then we'll be married. Let's do it right away.

TOU NGO *ignores him.*

TOU NGO:

> Are you not ashamed, mother?
> My father-in-law trudged from city to city all over the land,
> Striving to ensure that his family lacked nothing.
> When I think of all that my father-in-law acquired,
> I can't bear to think it should all be Donkey Chang's to enjoy.

DONKEY CHANG *gets hold of* TOU NGO *and tries to make her kneel;* TOU NGO *pushes him and he falls.*

> This is not what becomes of a woman when her husband is dead.

MOTHER TS'AI: Don't feel downhearted, sir. It's unthinkable that I should not repay your kindness in saving my life. It is only my daughter-in-law, she is difficult and touchy. She does not want your son for a husband, so how can I have you as mine? You and your son stay here in my house and

I'll provide you with good wine and good food, and let me win over my daughter-in-law gradually. Wait till she comes to her senses, then everything can be settled.

DONKEY CHANG [*to* TOU NGO]: You bitch! Even if you're a virgin, I hardly even touched you. You didn't have to fly into a temper and push me to the ground for nothing. Am I meant to take it lying down? I swear to your face, if I don't make you my wife I'm not a man. *Exeunt.*

ACT TWO

Enter DR LU.

DR LU:

I am a doctor if you ask me my trade,
I don't know how many I've helped on their way.
I never bother if people sue me in court,
I just shut up my shop for the day.

It was the weakness of the moment that made me try and strangle Mother Ts'ai. When the two men appeared I got such a fright that I dropped the rope and ran for it as fast as my legs would carry me. Although the whole night nothing happened, all the time I was jumpy and nervous. Then it struck me that a man's life is the concern of Heaven and Earth, how can I treat it as though it were a speck of dust on the wall! From now on I'll change my profession and atone for my sins. For each person I've killed I'll have a sutra said. Best Physician Lu, that's who I am. If Mother Ts'ai comes again, how am I to face her? How true the old saying is, 'Of the thirty-six ways of dealing with a crisis, the best is to run away.' I am glad I'm a bachelor. I'd better pack a few things up in a bundle, and lie low in some other place. I'll take up another profession and start again with a clean slate. What a relief that'll be!

Enter DONKEY CHANG.

DONKEY CHANG: Tou Ngo won't fall in with my scheme at all. The old woman has been taken ill. I'll buy some poison, and after I've poisoned the old woman the young one'll have to become my wife. [DONKEY CHANG *walks about.*] Wait! The city is full of prying eyes and wagging tongues. When they see me buying poison there's bound to be a commotion. The other day I saw a chemist's shop outside the South Gate. That's a quiet spot. That'll be the place to buy some. [*walks up to the shop*] I want to buy some medicine, doctor.

DR LU: What sort of medicine do you want?

DONKEY CHANG: I want to buy some poison.

DR LU: Who would dare to sell you poison? What a bold fellow you are!

DONKEY CHANG: Do you mean you won't sell me any?

DR LU: I won't. And what will you do about it?

DONKEY CHANG [*dragging* DR LU *with him*]: Very well. The other day you tried to murder Mother Ts'ai. Wasn't that you? You think I don't recognize you! I'm marching you straight off to the police.

DR LU [*frightened*]: If you let me go, I'll let you have some poison.

DR LU *gives him some poison.*

DONKEY CHANG: As you've given me the poison, I'll spare you this time. *Exit.*

DR LU: What bad luck! It would happen! Here I am giving him poison and if anything happens later I'll be involved in it more deeply than ever. While there's still time I'll close down the shop, and go to Cho-chou and sell rat-poison.

Exit.

Enter MOTHER TS'AI, *ill; she sits down at a table resting her head on her hands; enter* OLD CHANG *and* DONKEY CHANG.

OLD CHANG: Mother Ts'ai has kept me and my son in her house for some time now. She says that a marriage mustn't be hurried, and that she'll eventually persuade her daughter-in-law to come round. Now she's fallen ill herself. Haven't you had our fortunes read, son? When are these marriages that Heaven intends for us going to take place?

DONKEY CHANG: Had our fortunes read! Heaven intends! It's more a question of whether you yourself have got the guts to carry out your plans.

OLD CHANG: Mother Ts'ai has been ill for several days. Let's go and see how she is now. [*They see* MOTHER TS'AI.] How are you today, Mother Ts'ai?

MOTHER TS'AI: I'm in a very bad way.

OLD CHANG: Is there anything you'd like to eat or drink?

MOTHER TS'AI: I have a fancy for some mutton soup.

OLD CHANG: Go and tell Tou Ngo, son, to make some mutton soup for Mother Ts'ai.

DONKEY CHANG [*speaks in the direction of the doorway*]: Mother Ts'ai wants some mutton soup, Tou Ngo. Make some quickly, and bring it here.

TOU NGO *brings the soup.*

TOU NGO [*to* MOTHER TS'AI]: You and I are widows, mother. Whatever we do we must try to avoid arousing other people's suspicions. How can we keep Donkey Chang and his father here living under the same roof as us? They are not relations. [*aside*] I'm afraid there's no knowing what this woman will do.

The earth on the grave is not yet dry
And the dresses on her stand are changed for new.
How lamentable! Blush for shame!
Women! how faithless they have ever been,
Always ready to elope,
No will of their own,
A reproach in every way upon the wives of old –
And needless to say their nature cannot be changed.

The mutton soup is ready, mother. Here you are, have some.

DONKEY CHANG: Let me take it to her. [*He tastes the soup.*] It needs a little salt and vinegar. Go and get some.

TOU NGO *goes;* DONKEY CHANG *puts poison into the soup;* TOU NGO *re-enters.*

TOU NGO: Here is the salt and vinegar.

DONKEY CHANG: You put some in.

OLD CHANG: Have you got the mutton soup, son?

DONKEY CHANG: Yes. You take it over to her.

OLD CHANG [*gives the soup to* MOTHER TS'AI]: Here is the soup, mother. Drink up.

MOTHER TS'AI: I'm much obliged to you. [*makes as if to vomit*] I feel sick. I don't want any soup just now. You drink it, sir.

OLD CHANG: This soup was specially prepared for you. Even if you don't feel like drinking it all, have just a sip, mother.

MOTHER TS'AI: I don't want any. Please drink it yourself, sir.

OLD CHANG *drinks.*

TOU NGO:

> One says, Please drink,
> The other, Mother, you first.
> I cannot listen to such talk!
> I am beyond anger.

OLD CHANG: Why do I feel dizzy and faint after drinking the soup?

OLD CHANG *falls.*

MOTHER TS'AI [*alarmed*]: Wake up, sir! Come along! [*weeps*] He is dead.

TOU NGO:

> You had better listen to me.
> Admit it's your bad luck.
> See he's given a coffin
> And a few cotton clothes.
> When everything's ready send him out of the house,
> And bury him in another's graveyard, not ours.
> He was not the husband you wed in your youth,
> He was no relation of mine.
> I haven't a single sad tear to shed.
> Don't go breaking your heart
> Or losing your head
> So to sigh and wail
> And weep and sob.

DONKEY CHANG: Well, you've poisoned my father. What are you going to do about it?

MOTHER TS'AI: How is this all going to end, child?

TOU NGO: How should I have poison? It's his doing. When he asked me to fetch salt and vinegar, it was he who put poison in the soup.

DONKEY CHANG: My own father? You say that I, his son, have poisoned my father? Who will believe you? [*shouts*] Neighbours, listen! Tou Ngo has poisoned my father.

MOTHER TS'AI: Stop that! What a hullabaloo! You're frightening me out of my wits.

DONKEY CHANG: So you're frightened?

MOTHER TS'AI: Of course I'm frightened.

DONKEY CHANG: Do you want to be spared?

MOTHER TS'AI: Of course I want to be spared.

DONKEY CHANG: Then tell Tou Ngo to do what I say and address me three times as 'Dearest husband'. Then I'll spare you.

MOTHER TS'AI: Do what he says, child.

TOU NGO: How can you ask me to do this?

> No horse is made to bear a second saddle.
> Think of my husband and the two years we were man and wife.
> And now you would make me marry another.
> It can never be done.

DONKEY CHANG: You've poisoned my father, Tou Ngo. Do you want to settle it in court or out of court?

TOU NGO: What do you mean 'settle it in court or out of court'?

DONKEY CHANG: If you want to settle in court, I'll take you there to be tried and cross-examined and put to the torture. With a delicate body like yours you'll find it hard to bear that. You're bound to confess to having poisoned my father. If you want to settle out of court, you'd better become my wife just as quick as you can. It'll be doing you a favour.

TOU NGO: I have not poisoned your father. I'll go to court with you.

DONKEY CHANG *drags* TOU NGO *and* MOTHER TS'AI *off.* *Enter* PREFECT EVILBRUTE *with* ATTENDANTS.

PREFECT EVILBRUTE:

I am a magistrate, the best on the bench.
My coffers are filled from the cases I hear.
When any inspector comes to check on my files,
I'm to be found at home too sick to appear.

I am the Prefect Evilbrute of Ch'u-chou. The court is now in session. Come, men, raise your shout!

The ATTENDANTS *shout;*[1] DONKEY CHANG *drags in* TOU NGO *and* MOTHER TS'AI.

DONKEY CHANG: I'm bringing a charge! I'm bringing a charge!

ATTENDANT: Proceed.

DONKEY CHANG *kneels and* PREFECT EVILBRUTE *also kneels.*

ATTENDANT [*to* PREFECT]: Please get up, Your Honour! He is the one who is bringing the charge. Why are you kneeling to him?

PREFECT EVILBRUTE: Don't you know! Anyone who brings a case before me is father and mother to me; it is he who clothes and feeds me. [*rises*] Who is the accuser, and who the accused? Speak the truth, and nothing but the truth.

DONKEY CHANG: I am the accuser, my name is Donkey Chang. I accuse this woman, Tou Ngo, of putting poison into some mutton soup and killing my father. This is

Mother Ts'ai, my stepmother. I beg Your Honour to see justice done.

PREFECT EVILBRUTE: Who put in the poison?

TOU NGO: I had nothing to do with it.

MOTHER TS'AI: I had nothing to do with it either.

DONKEY CHANG: I had nothing to do with it either.

PREFECT EVILBRUTE: So nobody did it. Then it must have been me who put the poison in.

TOU NGO: My mother-in-law is not his stepmother. His name is Chang and our name is Ts'ai. One day my mother-in-law went to collect a debt from a certain Dr Lu. He took her outside the city and attempted to strangle her, but she was saved by this man and his father. She took the two of them home and gave them food and lodging, intending to do so as long as they lived out of gratitude for their kindness. Then suddenly these two took a wicked plan into their heads and started to claim that my mother-in-law was the younger one's stepmother so as to force me into becoming his wife. I am a married woman and not yet out of mourning. I refused to consent. It happened that my mother-in-law fell ill, and she asked me to prepare some mutton soup for her. I didn't know that Donkey Chang had any poison, nor do I know where he got it from, but he took the soup and said straightaway that it needed some more salt and vinegar. He sent me away on the pretext of fetching some and put the poison into the soup. It's only by Heaven's happy intervention that my mother-in-law suddenly began to feel sick, and not wanting any soup she let his father have it instead. After a few sips he died. I had nothing to do with it. I only hope Your Honour will exercise your great wisdom and see that justice is done to my case.

DONKEY CHANG: Will Your Honour please consider this?

Their name is Ts'ai. Our name is Chang. If her mother-in-law had not made my father her husband, why should she entertain us in her home? This woman may be young but she is extremely cunning and stubborn. Not even a beating would frighten her.

PREFECT EVILBRUTE: Human beings are low and cunning worms. Unless you beat them, they never confess. Come, take a thick rod and beat her.

An ATTENDANT *beats* TOU NGO*; three times she faints and is revived by water being splashed on her.*

TOU NGO:

> I cannot bear any more of this merciless rod.
> Mother, this is all of your doing.
> Ah, who is that shouting and roaring?
> I cannot help fainting and falling.
> A brief reprieve,
> Only to stir
> And swoon again.
> Another stroke,
> A streak of blood,
> A strip of skin.
> Where could I get poison, a woman like me?
> Heaven!
> Under an upturned bowl the sun never shines.

PREFECT EVILBRUTE: Are you going to confess or not?

TOU NGO: It was not I who put in the poison. That is the truth.

PREFECT EVILBRUTE: Since you didn't do it, someone go and beat the old woman.

TOU NGO [*hastily*]: Stop, stop, stop! Don't beat my mother-in-law. I am willing to confess. It was I who poisoned my father-in-law.

PREFECT EVILBRUTE: Now she's confessed, make her draw a cross on her statement. Put a cangue about her neck and take her to the death-cell. Tomorrow I shall pronounce sentence on her and she shall be escorted to the market-place to be beheaded.

MOTHER TS'AI [*weeps*]: It is I who am sending you to your death. It breaks my heart.

TOU NGO:

> I shall become a headless ghost burdened by injustice.
> How shall I ever let you go, you lecherous, licentious,
> shameless villain!
> Be sure the human heart is not to be deceived;
> All deeds of injustice are known to Heaven and Earth.
> I have fought to the end,
> Contested to the last.
> Now what am I to do?
> Mother,
> If I do not die,
> How am I to save you?

Exeunt TOU NGO, MOTHER TS'AI *and* ATTENDANTS.

DONKEY CHANG [*kowtows to the* PREFECT]: My thanks to Your Honour. Your judgement is the judgement of Heaven. When Tou Ngo is beheaded tomorrow my father will be avenged.

PREFECT EVILBRUTE: Beat the drum! The court is dismissed.

Exeunt.

ACT THREE

Enter the PRISON GOVERNOR.

PRISON GOVERNOR: I am the prison governor. There's to be an execution today. I've had policemen placed at every street corner to stop any unnecessary comings and goings.

Enter a POLICEMAN, *beating a drum and striking a gong three times; enter* TOU NGO *carrying the cangue escorted by the* EXECUTIONER *carrying a sword and waving a flag.*

EXECUTIONER: Get a move on, get a move on! The prison governor's already been at the execution ground some time now.

TOU NGO:

Without knowing I have violated the laws of the land,
Without any defence I am to meet with this punishment.
I cry Injustice! let Earth be moved, let Heaven quake!
Soon my spirit will descend to the deep all-embracing
Palace of Death.
How can Heaven and Earth not make complaint!
There the sun and moon hang by day and night,
There the spirits and gods dispense life and death.
Heaven and Earth!
It is for you to distinguish between right and wrong,
What confusion makes you mistake a villain for a saint?
The good suffer poverty and want, and their lives are
cut short;
The wicked enjoy wealth and honour, and always live
long.
Heaven and Earth!

You do but fear the strong and cheat the weak,
You too take the boat the current favours.
Earth! you cannot distinguish good and evil, can you yet be Earth!
Heaven! who mistake the fool for the sage, you are Heaven in vain!
Oh, nothing is left to me now but two streams of flowing tears.

EXECUTIONER: Hurry up! It's late.

TOU NGO:

With this cangue twisting me I turn this way and that,
With this crowd pressing me I fall forwards and back.

Sir, I would speak a word with you.

EXECUTIONER: What is it you want?

TOU NGO:

To go through the main streets is a great torment to me;
If we go by the back streets I shall die without complaint.
Don't make the excuse that it is longer that way.

EXECUTIONER: When you reach the execution ground is there any member of your family you would like to see? I can have him or her sent for. They will be allowed to see you once more.

TOU NGO:

Alas, I have only my shadow left to me now,
And to suffer in silence and cast sighs to the wind.

EXECUTIONER: Can it be possible that you don't even have a father or mother?

TOU NGO: I've only a father. Thirteen years ago he went to the capital to sit for the imperial examination. Ever since there's been no news of him.

EXECUTIONER: Just a moment ago you asked me to go through the back streets. Why?

TOU NGO:

> I fear that in the main street I may be seen by my
> mother-in-law.

EXECUTIONER: Your life is not your own now, why should you be afraid of being seen by her?

TOU NGO: If my mother-in-law sees me in fetters carrying this cangue and being led to the execution ground to be put to the sword,

> It will serve no purpose but to break her heart,
> It will serve no purpose but to break her heart.
> Grant me this favour, I am about to die.

Enter MOTHER TS'AI *weeping.*

MOTHER TS'AI: Heaven! is this my daughter-in-law?

EXECUTIONER: Stand back, old woman.

TOU NGO: Since my mother-in-law has come, ask her to come here. There is something I would ask of her.

EXECUTIONER: You, old woman, come here. Your daughter-in-law has something to ask you.

MOTHER TS'AI: My heart is breaking, my child.

TOU NGO: They are taking me to the execution ground today, mother, to receive my punishment. From now on at every New Year Festival and on the first and fifteenth day of each month, if there is any rice left over, ladle out a small portion for me, and if there is any paper money[2] left unburned, burn a hundred sheets for me – for the sake of your dead child.

> Remember Tou Ngo condemned unjustly for another's crime,
> Remember Tou Ngo cruelly severed head from limb,
> Remember Tou Ngo and all she did about the home;
> Mother,
> For the sake of her who has no father or mother,
> Remember Tou Ngo who has served you all these years.
> At feast days set aside for me a bowl of cold rice,
> Go to my punished corpse and burn some paper money.
> Let this offering be made to give my soul release.

MOTHER TS'AI: Set your mind at rest, my child. I will remember.

TOU NGO:

> Mother, do not weep and wail any more,
> Nor be distressed or bitter.
> It is only that I, Tou Ngo, was born when neither season nor fortune were mine.

EXECUTIONER: Stand back, old woman. It's time now.

TOU NGO *kneels; the* EXECUTIONER *unlocks the cangue.*

TOU NGO [*to the* PRISON GOVERNOR]: Your Honour, there is something I would ask of you. If you will grant this last request of mine I will die without complaint.

PRISON GOVERNOR: What request? Name it.

TOU NGO: I would ask for a clean mattress to stand on and a long strip of thin white silk to be hung from a lance. If it is true that I have been unjustly condemned, when the sword strikes and my head falls not one drop of my warm blood will be spilled on the ground. The blood will flow up into the strip of white silk.

PRISON GOVERNOR: This I grant. It's nothing.

The EXECUTIONER *spreads a mattress and takes a length of white silk and hangs it on a lance.*

EXECUTIONER: Is there anything else you want to say to His Honour? This is your last chance.

TOU NGO: Now is the hottest period of the summer, Your Honour. If it is true that I am unjustly condemned, when I die Heaven will send down a winter snow three feet deep to cover my corpse.

PRISON GOVERNOR: At the very height of summer? Even if your sentence were unjust and an offence against Heaven, you will never be able to summon down a single flake of snow. Don't talk nonsense.

TOU NGO:

> Heaven will be moved, be sure, and snow will fall like whirling flock,
> So that my corpse shall not lie exposed.
> What do I want with a white hearse and white horses[3]
> To carry me out to the ancient wastes.

It is true I have been unjustly condemned, Your Honour. And for three years to come the county of Ch'u shall suffer a drought.

PRISON GOVERNOR: Strike her mouth, someone! How dare you say that!

TOU NGO:

> You say nothing is to be expected of the Lord of Heaven,
> That there is no pity for the human heart.

You cannot know the Emperor of Heaven will fulfil
man's wishes.
Why for three years was no sweet rain seen to fall?
Only because in Tung-hai the virtuous Chou Ch'ing
had been wronged.
Now comes your turn in the city of Shan-yang,
All because you officials have no care to see justice done,
And anyone who has a mind to speak is forced to hold
his tongue.

The EXECUTIONER *waves his flag.*

EXECUTIONER: Why, the sky is suddenly clouding over. [*The sound of wind is heard offstage.*] What a cold wind!

TOU NGO:

For me the flying clouds grow dark,
For me the mournful wind begins to whirl.
The three prophecies shall be fulfilled for all to see.

[*weeps*] Wait, mother, and you will see snow fall in June and three years of drought.

Then will be revealed the injustice done to Tou Ngo.

The EXECUTIONER *swings his sword;* TOU NGO *falls.*

PRISON GOVERNOR [*awestruck*]: Ah, it is really snowing. Can such a thing be possible!

EXECUTIONER: Usually when I cut off a head the ground is covered with fresh blood. But the blood of Tou Ngo has all flown up into the strip of white silk. Not a single drop has fallen to the ground. I'd never have believed it!

PRISON GOVERNOR: There must be injustice in this case.

Two of the prophecies have been fulfilled. Who can say whether the prophecy of three years' drought will not come true? We shall have to see. Don't wait until the snow stops. Take up the corpse and bear it back to Mother Ts'ai.

Shouts of 'Yes, sir'; the corpse is carried off. Exeunt.

ACT FOUR

Enter TOU T'IEN-CHANG *in official costume with* CHANG CH'IEN *and an* ATTENDANT.

TOU T'IEN-CHANG: It is sixteen years since I left my child Tuan-yün. When I arrived at the capital I sat for the imperial examination, passed and was made an assistant to the prime minister. Lately, thanks to the special grace of His Majesty, I have been promoted Inspector-General of the Huai River Valley. Wherever I go I pass sentence on prisoners, investigate records, and whenever I discover officials who are corrupt or misuse their authority I have power to execute them first and report afterwards. I am both happy and sad. Happy because I wear the imperial sword and carry the gold tablet of office; sad for my child Tuan-yün. When she was seven I gave her to become Mother Ts'ai's daughter-in-law. Since my appointment I have sent people to Ch'u-chou to ask after Mother Ts'ai. But her neighbours say she has moved elsewhere and nobody knows where she has gone. So far there is still no news. I have wept for my child till my eyes have grown dim and my grief has turned my hair white. Today I have come to a district south of the Huai River. For some reason there has been no rain in Ch'u-chou for three years. I have taken up my lodging here in the official residence of the county. Chang Ch'ien, tell the county officials they are excused today and that I'll see them early tomorrow morning. And tell the heads of the six departments to bring all their records here. I shall examine some under the lamp. [CHANG CH'IEN *brings in the records.*] Light the lamp, Chang Ch'ien. You're tired. Go and rest. Don't come unless I call. [CHANG CH'IEN *lights the lamp and goes out with the* ATTENDANT.] Let me look through some of these records. 'Prisoner Tou Ngo poisoned her father-in-law.' The first record I read and the prisoner happens to have the same name as mine. To poison one's father-in-law is one of the ten unpardonable crimes. So there are people bearing the same name as me who have no respect for the law. This case has already been concluded, I am not going to read any more. I'll put it to the bottom of the pile and have a look at another. [*yawns*] I feel sleepy. It's because I am old, and tired from sitting so long in the saddle. Let me rest my head on the table for a while.

TOU T'IEN-CHANG *sleeps; enter the* GHOST OF TOU NGO.

GHOST OF TOU NGO:

Every day I watch and weep looking homeward from
my ghostly tower,
Impatiently I await my enemy.
Slowly as in a swoon I walk,
Swiftly as in the wind I come,
Though locked in mists and buried in cloud,
My ghostly spirit hastens me on.

[*looks forward*] The gods guarding the gate would not let me pass. But I said I was the daughter of Tou T'ien-chang, the

Inspector-General. I was unjustly condemned to death and my father does not know. I have come especially to appear to him in a dream. [*cries*] Father!

To what use were you given Imperial Sword and Gold Tablet?
See that my corpse three years decaying in an unjust death
Be delivered from the Boundless Sea of Bitterness.

The GHOST OF TOU NGO *comes forward, looks at her father and weeps;* TOU T'IEN-CHANG *begins to weep.*

TOU T'IEN-CHANG: Tuan-yün, my child, where are you? [*The* GHOST OF TOU NGO *withdraws;* TOU T'IEN-CHANG *awakes.*] Extraordinary! I had hardly closed my eyes when I dreamed that I saw my child Tuan-yün coming to me. Where can she be? Let me go on reading these records. [*The* GHOST OF TOU NGO *darkens the lamp.*] Strange! When I am about to look at these cases, why should the lamp begin to flicker? Chang Ch'ien has gone to bed, I shall have to trim the candle myself. [TOU T'IEN-CHANG *trims the candle; the* GHOST OF TOU NGO *shifts the records.*] There, that's the candle trimmed. It's bright enough now. Let me look at another case or two. 'Prisoner Tou Ngo poisoned her father-in-law.' [*surprised*] I've read this record before and put it at the bottom of the pile. How does it come to be on top still? This case has already been dealt with and goes to the bottom of the pile. Now let me look at another. [*The* GHOST OF TOU NGO *darkens the lamp.*] The lamp is going dim again. I'll have to trim it again. [TOU T'IEN-CHANG *trims the candle; the* GHOST OF TOU NGO *again shifts the records.*] There, that's the candle trimmed again. It's bright enough now. Let me look at another case. 'Prisoner Tou Ngo poisoned her father-in-law.' Hm, this is most extraordinary! I'm certain I put this record at the bottom just now. How does it come to be on top again each time I trim the candle? Can there be a ghost at the back of the hall here? Even if there's no ghost, there must have been some injustice in this case. I'll put this record to the bottom again. Now let me look at another. [*The* GHOST OF TOU NGO *again darkens the lamp.*] How is it that the lamp grows dim again? Is it possible that a ghost can be tampering with it? I'll trim it again. [TOU T'IEN-CHANG *trims the candle; the* GHOST OF TOU NGO *comes forward and confronts him;* TOU T'IEN-CHANG *draws his sword and strikes it on the table.*] There is a ghost, I say! You, ghost! I am an Inspector-General with the Gold Tablet, a personal representative of the Emperor. Come out, and I'll cut you in two with one stroke of my sword! Chang Ch'ien, are you still asleep? Get up quickly! There's a ghost, there's a ghost! Do you expect me not to be frightened?

GHOST OF TOU NGO:

> See how wildly he cries out in his confusion.
> At the sound of my weeping he shudders and quakes.
> Oh, Tou T'ien-chang, how awesome is your power now!
> Allow your daughter Tou Ngo to kowtow to you.

TOU T'IEN-CHANG: You, ghost, you say allow my daughter Tou Ngo to kowtow to me. You are clearly mistaken. My daughter is called Tuan-yün. You say you are called Tou Ngo. How can you be my daughter?

GHOST OF TOU NGO: After you had given me to Mother Ts'ai she changed my name to Tou Ngo.

TOU T'IEN-CHANG: If you are my daughter let me ask you one question. Was it you who poisoned your father-in-law in this case?

GHOST OF TOU NGO: It was your child.

TOU T'IEN-CHANG: Say no more, wretch! I have cried for you till my eyes have grown dim and grieved till my hair has turned white. You have committed one of the ten most atrocious crimes and suffered the penalty. When I gave you to be married into their family I charged you to observe the Three Duties and the Four Virtues.[4] You did nothing of the kind. For three generations not one male member of the Tou family has violated the law, and for five generations not one female has married again. But now you have disgraced your ancestors and endangered my reputation. Tell me the whole truth this instant. Utter the slightest lie and I shall have you arrested[5] and sent to the Temple of the City God, where you will never be born a human being again but will remain for ever condemned to be a hungry ghost on the Mountain of Shadows.

GHOST OF TOU NGO: Restrain your anger, father. Listen to your child. I had been married to my husband for two years when he died. One day a Dr Lu, who owed her a debt of twenty taels of silver, attempted to strangle my mother-in-law. She was saved by a certain Chang and his son Donkey, who, knowing she had a widowed daughter-in-law at home, said that since she and I had no husbands it would be a good idea if we married his father and him. If she didn't agree, he said he would strangle her as the other one had tried to. My mother-in-law took fright and felt obliged to make them certain vague promises. She took them home intending to support them for the rest of their lives. Several times Donkey Chang tried to take advantage of me but I firmly refused. One day my mother-in-law fell ill and asked for some mutton soup, so I prepared some. Just then Donkey Chang and his father came in to ask after her health. Donkey Chang asked to taste the soup. He said it was delicious but needed a little more salt and vinegar. He sent me to get some and took the opportunity to put in some poison without being seen, fully expecting that once my mother-in-law was dead he could force me to marry him. Suddenly without any warning my mother-in-law began to feel sick, and refusing the soup, offered it to Old Chang. He drank it and instantly died from the poison. Donkey Chang turned and said I killed his father; did I intend to settle it in court or out of court? If I wished it to be in court he would accuse me there and demand my life for his father's; if out of court, it would have to be as his wife. I told him that a horse cannot bear a second saddle nor a good wife take a second husband; I would rather die than marry him, and would go with him to court. He took me to court, and there I was beaten, and though they tried to kill me I would not admit that it was I who committed the crime. When the magistrate saw that I would not weaken he threatened to beat my mother-in-law. My mother-in-law is old and could not stand up to a beating, so I was forced into making a confession. I was escorted to the execution ground to be beheaded, and there before the face of Heaven I made three prophecies.

Read this record, does it not confirm what I say?
This injustice calls for patience, but how can I be
  patient?
I would not yield obedience to another,
Yet this brought me to the execution ground;

I would not bring disgrace upon my ancestors,
Yet this cost me the remainder of my days.
Oh, set up a tower today for the repose of my soul,
For a soul grieving in injustice.
Father, the Emperor's powers are vested in you,
Examine this record with care.
That violator of all natural custom deserves to be undone.
If the villain were cut into ten thousand pieces,
It were not revenge enough to satisfy my soul.

TOU T'IEN-CHANG [*weeps*]: Oh, my child, so wrongly put to death! This will break my heart. But let me ask you, is it because of you that for three years now no rain has fallen in Ch'u-chou?

GHOST OF TOU NGO: It is because of me.

TOU T'IEN-CHANG: Can such a thing be possible! When tomorrow comes you shall have justice. I fear the dawn is breaking. Go now. Tomorrow I shall have the record put right. [*Exit the* GHOST OF TOU NGO.] Ah, the day breaks. [*Enter* CHANG CH'IEN.] Last night, Chang Ch'ien, while I was reading the records a ghost came complaining of injustice. Several times I called out to you but you never answered me. You stayed sound asleep.

CHANG CH'IEN: I haven't slept a wink. I didn't hear any ghost come complaining of injustice. I didn't hear you calling me.

TOU T'IEN-CHANG [*declares*]: The court is now in session.

CHANG CH'IEN: The Magistrate of the County asks to be received.

Enter the MAGISTRATE OF THE COUNTY.

CHANG CH'IEN: The Chief of Police asks to be received.

Enter the CHIEF OF POLICE.

TOU T'IEN-CHANG: Here in your county of Ch'u-chou there has been no rain for three years. Do you know why?

MAGISTRATE: It is due to this dry weather. It's a disaster for the people of Ch'u-chou. We don't know who is to blame.

TOU T'IEN-CHANG [*angrily*]: You don't know who is to blame! There was a woman, Tou Ngo, in the city of Shan-yang, convicted for poisoning her father-in-law. Before she was beheaded she made a prophecy: that if there had been injustice done in her case, for three years no rain would fall in Ch'u-chou, not an inch of grass would grow. Was there not such a case?

MAGISTRATE: The case was heard before the now promoted Prefect of Tao-chou. The record is there.

TOU T'IEN-CHANG: Such a muddle-headed official must have found promotion difficult. You are his successor. Within these three years have you made sacrifices to the spirit of this unjustly condemned woman?

MAGISTRATE: The crime she committed was one of the ten most atrocious crimes. There could be no temple erected and dedicated to her. So we have not.

TOU T'IEN-CHANG: In the Han dynasty there was a certain widow whose mother-in-law committed suicide. Her sister-in-law accused her of killing her mother and the Prefect of Tung-hsi had the woman beheaded. Because of the injustice done to this woman rain did not fall for three years. Afterwards when Judge Yü was inspecting the prison records he saw this woman in a vision come clasping her record weeping before the court. The judge set the record right, and went in person to make sacrifices to the woman at her tomb. At once a heavy rain began to fall. Today there is a drought in your county of Ch'u-chou; does this not resemble that case? Order the police to go to the city of Shan-yang and arrest Donkey Chang, Dr Best Physician Lu and Mother Ts'ai. Bring them here to court without another moment's delay.

Exeunt the MAGISTRATE OF THE COUNTY, *the* CHIEF OF POLICE *and* CHANG CH'IEN.
Re-enter CHANG CH'IEN *with a* PRISON WARDER *escorting* DONKEY CHANG *and* MOTHER TS'AI.

CHANG CH'IEN: Prisoners from the city of Shan-yang waiting to be called.

TOU T'IEN-CHANG: Donkey Chang.

DONKEY CHANG: Here.

TOU T'IEN-CHANG: Mother Ts'ai.

MOTHER TS'AI: Here.

TOU T'IEN-CHANG: Why is Dr Lu, one of the principal offenders, not here?

PRISON WARDER: Dr Lu fled the city three years ago. A warrant has been issued for his arrest.

TOU T'IEN-CHANG: Is Mother Ts'ai your stepmother, Donkey Chang?

DONKEY CHANG: Indeed! Does one call a woman mother on false pretences?

TOU T'IEN-CHANG: This poison must have come from some chemist's shop. Tou Ngo was a young widow, how could she obtain poison? It must have been you who got the poison, Donkey Chang, didn't you?

DONKEY CHANG: Even if I got the poison, would I use it on my own father?

TOU T'IEN-CHANG: You, my child unjustly put to death, this is an important point in the case. If you do not appear and defend yourself how shall the truth be revealed? Where is your unhappy ghost?

Enter the GHOST OF TOU NGO.

GHOST OF TOU NGO: If you did not buy the poison, who did, Donkey Chang?

DONKEY CHANG [*shrinks back in terror*]: A ghost! A ghost! O Supreme Sage, work your spell! Put a pinch of salt in water! As quick as the quickest thunder-devil!

GHOST OF TOU NGO: You meant to poison my mother-in-law so that you could make me your wife by force. But my mother-in-law did not drink the soup; instead she let your father drink it and your father was poisoned. Do you still dare to deny it today?

The GHOST OF TOU NGO *beats* DONKEY CHANG; DONKEY CHANG *dodges.*

DONKEY CHANG: O Supreme Sage! Save me! As quick as the quickest thunder-devil! Your Honour said that the poison must have come from a chemist's shop. If the chemist who sold the poison can be found to bear witness against me, I shall go to my death without a word of complaint.

Enter another PRISON WARDER *escorting* DR LU.

PRISON WARDER: From the city of Shan-yang another prisoner, Dr Best Physician Lu.

CHANG CH'IEN [*to* DR LU]: Kneel down.

TOU T'IEN-CHANG: Three years ago you attempted to strangle Mother Ts'ai in order to acquit yourself of a debt of twenty taels of silver that you owed her. What have you to say?

DR LU [*kowtows to* TOU T'IEN-CHANG]: It is true that I tried to repudiate the debt I owed her. But she was saved by two men and came to no harm.

TOU T'IEN-CHANG: The two men, do you know their names?

DR LU: I would recognize them. In the confusion I didn't ask them their names.

TOU T'IEN-CHANG: There's one of them below there. Go and see if you recognize him.

DR LU [*looks about him*]: This is Mother Ts'ai. [DR LU *points at* DONKEY CHANG *and says, aside*] The business of the poison has been discovered. [*aloud*] This is one of them. Let me explain to Your Honour what happened. When I was trying to strangle Mother Ts'ai that day, this fellow appeared with his father and saved the woman. A few days later he came to my shop, asking for poison. I am a devout Buddhist and I'd never dare do anything that goes against my conscience. So I told him my shop only sold medicines approved by the government; none of your so-called poisons. He stared at me and said: 'You tried to strangle Mother Ts'ai the other day. I'm marching you straight off to the police.' Now the one thing I dread most of all in life is being brought face to face with an official, so there was nothing I could do but give him a small measure of poison. I could see that he had an evil face and was out to kill somebody with it. I knew the matter would be found out in the end and I'd be involved, so I escaped to the district of Cho-chou and took to selling rat poison. I have poisoned a lot of rats but I've never sold any poison to kill a human being again.

GHOST OF TOU NGO:

So you, Dr Lu, sold the poison and Donkey Chang bought it.
Magistrates may go, but the court remains.

TOU T'IEN-CHANG: Bring forward Mother Ts'ai. I see that you are over sixty and a woman of means. Why did you marry Old Chang?

MOTHER TS'AI: He and his son saved my life, so I decided to maintain them in comfort for the rest of their days. Donkey Chang often suggested that I should marry his father but I never promised to do so.

TOU T'IEN-CHANG: Under such circumstances your daughter-in-law should never have confessed that she poisoned her father-in-law.

GHOST OF TOU NGO: The examining magistrate of that time threatened to have my mother-in-law beaten. I was afraid that being old she would not be able to endure the punishment so I confessed that it was I who had poisoned my father-in-law. It was a confession forced upon me.

Ah, true it is, from ancient times courts face the South[6]
But not once within their walls is justice done.
What agony my delicate weak body suffers in its grave!
Three years already have long gone by
And still my sorrows flow onward like the long Huai river.

TOU T'IEN-CHANG: Now I know fully the injustice done to you, my child. Go now. I shall pass sentence on these prisoners and the magistrate who heard the case. Tomorrow

I shall have a sutra said for the deliverance of your soul to paradise.

The GHOST OF TOU NGO *kowtows to* TOU T'IEN-CHANG.

GHOST OF TOU NGO:

> Again Imperial Sword and Gold Tablet shall reveal
> their power,
> To break corrupt officials and abusers of place,
> To share the sorrows of the Son of Heaven,
> And to root out evil for the people's sake.

Father, I have forgotten one thing. My mother-in-law is well advanced in years and there is no one to look after her. Will you take her into your household and for my sake treat her as is her due? Then I shall be able to close my eyes at last beneath the Nine Streams.

TOU T'IEN-CHANG: What a dutiful child you are!

GHOST OF TOU NGO: And father, below my name, Tou Ngo,

> Revoke the sentence of conviction that caused my
> unjust death.

TOU T'IEN-CHANG: Call Mother Ts'ai forward. Do you recognize me?

MOTHER TS'AI: I am old and my eyesight's getting dim. No, I don't recognize you.

TOU T'IEN-CHANG: I am Tou T'ien-chang. The ghost that was here was my unjustly condemned daughter Tou Ngo. All here present, listen to the sentence of the court. Donkey Chang, for poisoning his own father and conspiring to rape a widow, let him first be quartered then beheaded. Prefect Evilbrute, now promoted Prefect of Tao-chou, and the Chief of Police, for conspiring to prevent the administration of justice, let them each be given a hundred strokes of the lash and be permanently dismissed from the service. Dr Lu, for attempting to repudiate a debt by strangling one of His Majesty's subjects, and for unlawfully selling poison so as to cause loss of life, let him be exiled for ever to the pestilential marshes of the South.

CHANG BOILS THE SEA

by

Li Hao-ku

(*early thirteenth century*)

CHANG BOILS THE SEA

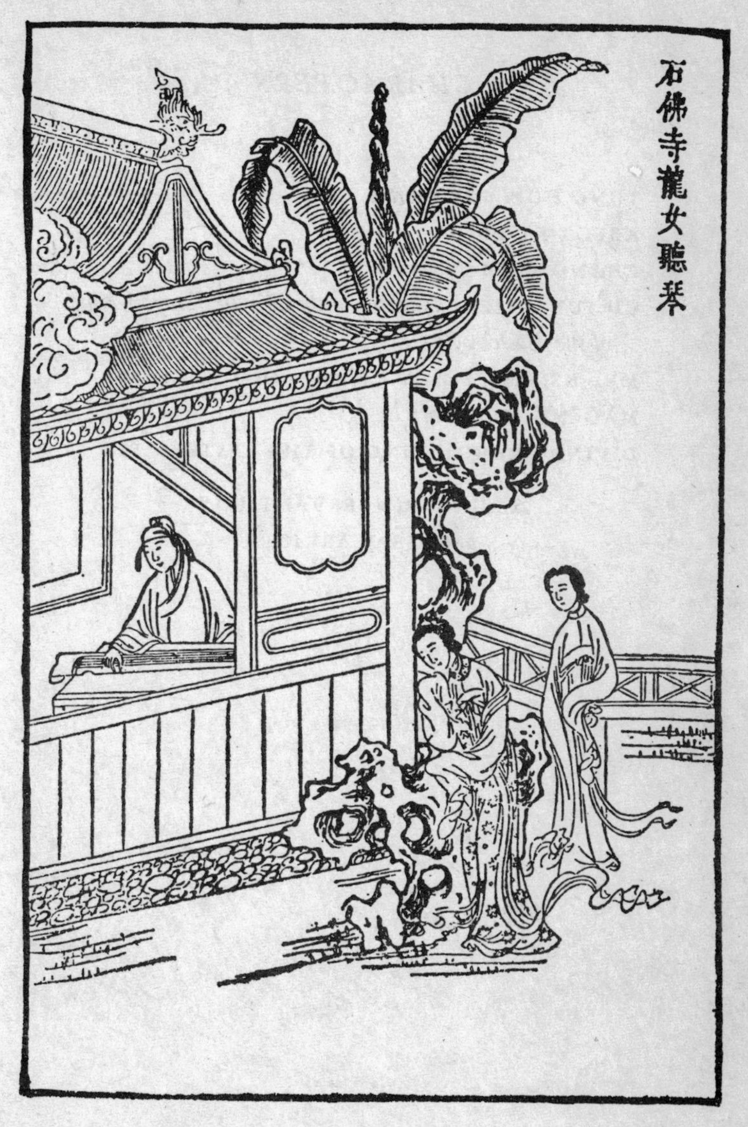

據明崇禎刻本柳枝集影印

CHARACTERS

TUNG HUA, *an immortal*

ABBOT FA YÜN

CHANG YÜ, *a student*

CH'IUNG-LIEN, *daughter to the Divine Dragon King of the Eastern Sea*

MEI-HSIANG, *maid to Ch'iung-lien*

MAO-NÜ, *an immortal*

DIVINE DRAGON KING OF THE EASTERN SEA

A RUNNER, *a* SERVANT BOY
and SEA-WARRIORS

CHANG BOILS THE SEA

ACT ONE

Enter TUNG HUA.

TUNG HUA: I am Tung Hua, an immortal of the Upper Rank. Once upon a time a Gold Immortal Page and a Jade Immortal Maiden fell in love with each other during the Festival of the Green Jasper Pool. Both were banished as a punishment to be born into the World of Mortals. The Gold Page was born a boy into a Chang family in Chaochou. He is widely read in the Confucian classics and has become quite a scholar. The Jade Maiden was born a girl in the house of the Divine Dragon King of the Eastern Sea. Not until they have repaid this ancient debt of love shall I bring them to their senses and lead them back to the Path of Immortality. *Exit.*

Enter ABBOT FA YÜN *with his* RUNNER.

ABBOT FA YÜN: I am Fa Yün, Abbot of the Temple of the Stone Buddha. This ancient temple of ours is situated on the shore of the Eastern Sea. Often the Dragon King and his sea-warriors come here for their amusement. Go out to the gate, runner, and send me word if you see any visitor coming.

RUNNER: Yes, your reverence.

Enter CHANG YÜ *and his* SERVANT BOY.

CHANG YÜ: I am Chang Yü. My parents died long ago. From

my childhood I have studied the classics quite diligently, and yet I don't know why, I have never been able to pass the imperial examination. Today I have nothing to do, so I have come to while away the time by the seashore. Look, an ancient temple, and a runner standing at the gate. Has this temple got a name, my man?

RUNNER: Got a name! A mountain without a name would be very confusing; a temple without a name would be too vulgar for words. This is the Temple of the Stone Buddha.

CHANG YÜ: Go and tell the abbot that a young student is here and wishes to pay his respects to him.

RUNNER: There's a young student at the gate. He wishes to pay his respects to you, master.

ABBOT: Ask him to come in. [*The* ABBOT *sees* CHANG YÜ.] Where do you come from, may I ask, master scholar?

CHANG YÜ: I am a native of Chao-chou. I saw what a quiet place your ancient temple was, and I hoped your reverence would let me have a room where I could revise my studies.

ABBOT: We have plenty of rooms in the temple. Runner, prepare a room in a quiet place somewhere in the south-east quarter so that the scholar can study.

CHANG YÜ: I've nothing else to offer your reverence but two taels of silver. Please accept it as a donation to the temple.

ABBOT: Since you so wish, I accept it. Get the room ready, runner, and prepare the scholar a meal. *Exeunt.*

Enter the RUNNER, CHANG YÜ *and his* SERVANT BOY.

RUNNER: We've given you this quiet room. Here you can turn somersaults, play football, dance a devil-dance, do any silly thing you can think of. Just please yourself, enjoy yourself! I'm off to the Hall of Meditation to wait on my master. *Exit.*

CHANG YÜ: The life the monks lead is peaceful and civilized; and no idlers about for ever making a noise. What a wonderful opportunity for me to study! It's getting dark. Bring the *ch'in*, boy. I'll play a tune or two to amuse myself. [*The* SERVANT BOY *places the* ch'in *on the table.*] Light the lamp and burn a joss-stick. [*The* SERVANT BOY *lights the lamp and burns a joss-stick.*]

I hope I shall not play in vain on themes of running
streams and lofty peaks;
With Chung Chi gone, how few are left of music's
connoisseurs!
Tonight beside the lamp I'll play a strain or two,
Perhaps a wandering fish may come out to listen.

Enter CH'IUNG-LIEN, *daughter to the* DRAGON KING, *with her maid,* MEI-HSIANG.

CH'IUNG-LIEN: I am Ch'iung-lien, the third daughter of the Divine Dragon King of the Eastern Sea. With my maid Mei-hsiang I have come to while away the evening walking on the seashore.

MEI-HSIANG: Look at the vast sea, how calm and clear it is! And the same colour as the great sweep of the sky. What a beautiful scene!

CH'IUNG-LIEN:

Look, rising from the sea, ten thousand brightly
coloured clouds,
And a wheel of bright moon glints among the waves.

MEI-HSIANG: Are the sights and scenes in the sea not the same as those in the world of mortals?

CH'IUNG-LIEN:

Look at the noblest palaces of the world of mortals,
How can they be compared with the Dragon Palaces of the Watery Realm,
So clear, so deep!
Heavenly caves and happy abodes where to live as we please,
So blue, so vast!
Never disturbed by babbling ducks or clamour of geese in flight.

MEI-HSIANG: I am sure between Heaven and Earth there can be hardly any comparison.

CH'IUNG-LIEN:

They are not to be compared; one sweep and the glories of the world of men are gone,
Like autumn grass in a whirl of dust.
Spring passes, summer comes; autumn, then winter again.
They hear now the crow of the dawn-heralding cock,
Now the tick of the night-measuring clock,
Never thinking it is their lives that they fritter away.

CHANG YÜ *plays the* ch'in*;* MEI-HSIANG *listens.*

MEI-HSIANG: Where does that sound come from?

CH'IUNG-LIEN:

Listen, the evening breeze stirring,
A wind descending on ten thousand pines,
The splash of river rushing,
Water falling down a sheer gorge.
It is not the lotus-gathering girls plying their oars,

Nor the fisherman beating a plank at the stern,
It would arouse the night sleeper from heavy-eyed sleep.

MEI-HSIANG: The sound is quite unlike any other.

CH'IUNG-LIEN:

It is not the dangling jade trinkets'
Rhythmic tinkling,
Nor the jostling iron horses[1]
Jangling in the eaves,
Nor from priest's temple cell
Beating of stone *ch'ing*[2] or bell.
Each note disturbs me, sets my heart trembling.
Why, it is the sound of strings!
Who can be playing the *ch'in*?

CHANG YÜ *plays on.*

MEI-HSIANG: It must be someone in the temple making the noise.

CH'IUNG-LIEN: It's someone playing the *ch'in*.

MEI-HSIANG: Listen!

CH'IUNG-LIEN:

There is endless emotion in phrase after phrase;
Note after note the tune goes on and on,
Like trembling gold chrysanthemums the autumn wind stirs,
Like the fragrance of *kuei*[3] the autumn wind carries,
Like emerald bamboo swaying where the autumn wind dallies.
I, ya, ya!
Like gold-thread shuttle travelling the loom of brocade,
Ti, lu, lu!

Like pearls slipping from a woman's hand dancing and sparkling.

MEI-HSIANG *steals a glance at* CHANG YÜ.

MEI-HSIANG: It's a student playing the *ch'in* here. What a splendid young man!

CH'IUNG-LIEN:

The strings express his inmost thoughts,
His fingers his dexterity.
More than *p'i pa*, slowly plucking, softly sweeping
It speaks of his true nature and his outward grace,
His face a Taoist's, his bearing like a god's.
Despite myself it stirs my deepest feelings.

MEI-HSIANG: You who understand music are bound to be moved. Even I find the strains of his music very pleasant on the ear. Certainly he plays well.

CH'IUNG-LIEN:

Truly he is gifted,
Nay, his art is near divine,
Expressing sadness like a singing swan,
Intensity like a winter cricket,
Delicacy like a flower's face,
Majesty like the thunder's roll –
Music to dispel ten thousand forms of idle sorrow!
A scholar so excellent in this one thing
Must excel in a hundred more.
I have tiptoed here, stealing each step.
He moves from mood to mood.
How much more their power over me than the poems of P'an-pan over Huang T'ing-chien![4]

Like a wonderful night upon one pillow wandering
 one immortal dream.

A string snaps.

CHANG YÜ: Why has the string suddenly snapped? There must be someone listening secretly. I shall go out and look.

CH'IUNG-LIEN *draws back.*

CH'IUNG-LIEN: What a handsome young man!

CHANG YÜ *sees her.*

CHANG YÜ: What a lovely young woman! May I ask, lady, what family you are from and why you are wandering abroad in the night?

CH'IUNG-LIEN:

My home is in realms of azure cloud
And in the midst of green waves,
Attended by those who wear scales and horns.
Deep in the rich Palace of Crystals I live,
Daughter of a sea-dweller, one Dragon by name,
Surpassing even the immortal maid Hsü Fei-ch'iung.[5]
Do all stars not gather in homage round the North Star?
Do all rivers not pay their tribute to the Eastern Sea?

CHANG YÜ: Your name is Dragon. I remember there's such a name in the Book of Surnames. So, gentle lady, you have a surname. Have you no other? What brings you here?

CH'IUNG-LIEN: I am the third daughter of Mr Dragon and my name is Ch'iung-lien. I heard you playing the *ch'in* so I came to listen.

CHANG YÜ: If you come to listen to the *ch'in* you must love and understand music very well. Why not come into my study and I will play a piece for you? Will you?

CH'IUNG-LIEN: Willingly. [CH'IUNG-LIEN *enters the study.*] May I ask you your name, sir?

CHANG YÜ: My name is Chang Yü, I am a native of Chao-chou. My parents died when I was young. I've studied very hard at the classics but somehow I've never been able to pass the imperial examination. In the course of studying and travelling I've arrived here. I have no wife.

MEI-HSIANG: What impudence this scholar has! Who asked whether you had a wife or not?

SERVANT BOY: It's not only my master who hasn't a wife; I haven't got a wife either.

CHANG YÜ: If you don't mind being poor, will you become my wife?

CH'IUNG-LIEN: You are gifted and clever, handsome and wise. With all my heart I will become your wife. But I have parents and I must ask them. On the fifteenth day of the eighth month, at the Mid-autumn Festival, come to our home and they will receive you formally as their son-in-law.

CHANG YÜ: Since you consent, surely it would be best if we were married tonight. How wonderful that would be! How can I wait until the Mid-autumn Festival?

SERVANT BOY: That's true! I can't wait either.

MEI-HSIANG: You can't wait! That's easily settled.

CH'IUNG-LIEN: The proverb has it, 'Time is nothing where love is concerned.' Why can't you wait?

CHANG YÜ: May I ask where is your home?

CH'IUNG-LIEN:

> Only thirty thousand fathoms beneath the blue sea,
> And as perilous as the Twelve Peaks of Mount Wu.

CHANG YÜ: If you keep your word I'll be faithful and true.

CH'IUNG-LIEN:

> With sweet words you play with me, play with me,
> With smiling face you flatter me, flatter me.
> Watch for August's icy wheel to rise from east of the sea,
> Then the mists will withdraw, the skies be clear,
> Breezes waft through the bamboo screen;
> Then shall be the harmony of cloud and rain.
> Smiling you and I shall follow each other,
> Nor shall it be for only half a year.

CHANG YÜ: Since you've promised to be my wife, will you leave me something as a pledge?

CH'IUNG-LIEN: I have here a handkerchief woven from the silk of the ice silkworm. I've nothing better as a pledge of my love. Water will not wet it nor will it burn in fire.

CHANG YÜ: How can I thank you, dear lady!

SERVANT BOY: What will you give me as a pledge, Mei-hsiang?

MEI-HSIANG: I'll give you a broken rush-leaf fan. Take that home to fan your fire.

SERVANT BOY: Where will I find you?

MEI-HSIANG: Go to Brick Pagoda Street, at the corner of the Sheep Market, outside the entrance to the police station. Look for me there.

CH'IUNG-LIEN:

> Do you not know what it is when two hearts are one?
> Only a foolish heart would understand.
> I am not a demon devouring men,

Don't be alarmed or dismayed.
The destiny of our former lives shall be fulfilled in this,
At the Mid-autumn Festival our happiness shall be complete.
Rest assured!
Cast aside the ten thousand miles of mist and doubt,
Where I am all is tranquil,
With none of the cares of the World of Dust.

CHANG YÜ: I will come. [*Exeunt* CH'IUNG-LIEN *and* MEI-HSIANG.] This woman's beauty has bewitched me. There is none to compare with her in all the world. She tells me I must look for her by the seashore. I cannot wait till the Mid-autumn Festival. Look after my sword, my *ch'in* and my box of books, boy. With this handkerchief I am ready to dare anything. I'm going to the seashore to look for her. *Exit.*

SERVANT BOY: What a fool my master is! For all we know she might be a demon or a monster. He believes the first thing she says, and off he goes chasing after her. I'll tell the abbot and his runner and we'll catch him up. *Exit.*

ACT TWO

Enter CHANG YÜ.

CHANG YÜ: Where has she gone? I can see nothing but green hills and blue water, cypresses and pine-trees. I can't go any further, and I can't go back. O what misery! I'll rest awhile on that rock over there. [*Withdraws.*]

Enter MAO-NÜ.

MAO-NÜ:

> The mulberry field is now field, now sea.
> In a glance a hundred years go by.
> Turn your mind to higher things,
> And who will not gain immortality?

I was formerly a maidservant in the Palace of Ch'in. One day I went into a mountain to gather herbs, and ever after that I ate only uncooked food. Gradually my body became lighter and lighter, and so I attained the Great Way. I am known to the world as the immortal Mao-nü. Wandering at will today I chanced to come to this place, the eastern shore of the sea. What a great expanse of water!

> The bright brimming ice moon rises from the edge of the sea,
> The bright beaming red sun turns the mountain ridge.
> The sun and moon come and go,
> Only the mountains and the sea remain.
> Whatever the river, great or small,
> All that is water
> Returns to the sea.

CHANG YÜ [*comes forward*]: What place can this be? Oh, what luck! Here is a woman coming this way – a Taoist priestess. I will ask her. What is this place, may I ask, mother?

MAO-NÜ:

> Since you so ask,
> First tell me your reason.

CHANG YÜ: I have come here to look for my love. I don't know where she has gone.

MAO-NÜ: Who are you, young man, and where are you from?

CHANG YÜ: I am a native of Chao-chou. I have been travelling and studying. At the moment I am staying at the Temple of the Stone Buddha. Last night while I was playing the *ch'in* a woman and her maid came to listen. She told me she was the daughter of a certain Mr Dragon and that her name was Ch'iung-lien. And she promised to meet me on the seashore on the day of the Mid-autumn Festival. After she was gone I made my way to this place and suddenly I found myself lost. I thought her the most bewitching creature; there is not another like her in all the world.

MAO-NÜ: If she said her name was Dragon, had you no misgivings?

> Don't you know the women of the Dragon Palace are enchantresses?
> And are you willing to risk the remainder of your life
> All to incur a debt of love?
> The Dragon is a green-eyed god, is given to suspicion;
> His evil nature knows no bounds,
> In his malice he can work all forms of harm.

CHANG YÜ: Is he as wicked as that?

MAO-NÜ:

> Ah,
> When he shows his teeth and spreads his claws,
> And lightly lifts his horned head,
> In an instant he raises waves and billows,
> In another shakes the hills and mountains,
> In another rolls up the Yangtze and Huai rivers.
> When he grows large,

The universe is not large enough,
When small,
He can hide in a mustard seed.
He displays his strength,
Reveals his supernatural power,
Unleashes his venom at will.

CHANG YÜ: It is the woman's surname that is Dragon. Why do you start speaking of dragons, mother?

MAO-NÜ: Don't you know that the Dragon is not to be trifled with, young man?

He can raise clouds and mists,
In a trice they come,
Move winds and rain,
Stir storms of dust.
I fear a sudden cruel fright will lose you life and limb.
Do not keep your promise to love the Dragon's daughter,
And throw away your talents and your chance of fame and honour.

CHANG YÜ: Now I begin to understand. She is a daughter from the palace of a Dragon king, and her father is nothing but evil. How could he be willing to give his daughter to be my wife? The marriage is certainly out of the question. But Ch'iung-lien, what made you come and listen to my playing of the *ch'in*? [*downcast*]

MAO-NÜ: I am not an ordinary mortal. I have been sent by Tung Hua, an immortal of the Upper Rank, and commanded to bring you back to the Path of the True Way. He will not have you led astray.

CHANG YÜ *bows to* MAO-NÜ.

CHANG YÜ: My eyes are only mortal eyes and I did not recognize my counsellor for an immortal. I beg you to forgive me.

MAO-NÜ: That woman who came to listen to you playing the *ch'in* is the third daughter of the Dragon King of the Eastern Sea, and her name is Ch'iung-lien. She lives hidden in the Dragon Palace deep within the sea. How can you hope to find her?

CHANG YÜ: I believe that this daughter of the Dragon and I are destined to love each other.

MAO-NÜ: What makes you think this?

CHANG YÜ: If we were not destined to love each other how could she have been willing to ask me to go to her home on the night of the Mid-autumn Festival, and there be received as a son-in-law? What is more, she gave me this handkerchief as a pledge of her love.

MAO-NÜ: This handkerchief is certainly from the Dragon Palace. It is true then that the girl has fallen in love with you. But the Divine Dragon King is ill-tempered and violent. How will he be so ready to give his beloved daughter to be your wife? I will make the marriage possible for you by giving you three magic treasures. They will subdue him, sure enough. Then you need have no fear that he won't give his daughter to be married to you.

CHANG YÜ *kneels to* MAO-NÜ.

CHANG YÜ: I long to see your magic treasures, O immortal.

MAO-NÜ: Here I give you one silver pan, one gold coin, and one iron ladle.

CHANG YÜ *takes them from her.*

CHANG YÜ: I beg you, teach me how to use them best.

MAO-NÜ: Take this ladle and fill the pan with water out of the sea; into the water put the gold coin. Then boil the water down one tenth of an inch and the sea will drop one hundred feet; boil it down two tenths of an inch and the sea will drop two hundred feet; boil it till the pan is dry and there before you will be the bottom of the sea. How will the Divine Dragon King be able to go on living there then? He is bound to send someone to invite you to be his son-in-law.

CHANG YÜ: Thank you for your guidance, great immortal. But I don't know how far the seashore is from here.

MAO-NÜ: Go straight on some score of miles from here, and there you will come to the shore of the Island of the Gate of Sands.

These treasures,
From Purple Mansion and Jade Terrace they come, in realms of Purity and Light,
From the vast blue sphere of Heaven.
No matter how you carry out your task,
No matter what schemes you may devise,
Your heart's desires shall be fulfilled,
Its every passion gratified.
These treasures do not beg for favours,
Nor do they admit of bribes;
They will be your matchmakers,
And see you made a son-in-law,
Entwine you as branches of two different trees,
Unfold you as two flowers from a single stem,
Unite you as the twin phoenixes[6]
In the harmony of fish in stream.
Boil the vast sea dry! *Exeunt.*

ACT THREE

Enter the RUNNER.

RUNNER: Last night when our scholar was playing the *ch'in* he was bewitched and carried off by a spirit. His servant boy hurried off to look for him, and my master, without any thought for what he was doing, sent me out to look for him too. The forest was deep and the mountain path dangerous. Where was I to find him? Suddenly I came face to face with a tiger. He bared his teeth and waved his claws, then went for me. Quick as a flash I picked up a stone the size of a goose egg and threw it at him. I don't know how my aim could have been so steady, but the stone went right into his throat. I watched the animal struggle and collapse, and then in one breath I ran two hundred miles, and that's how I got away with my life and arrived here.

> One life's already bewitched and gone,
> But why should I die without good reason?
> Much better to follow the scholar and die
> An amorous ghost beneath a peony. *Exit.*

Enter CHANG YÜ *with his* SERVANT BOY.

CHANG YÜ: Here we are already at the seashore. Strike your flint and start the fire. Collect a few stones together to make a tripod and put the pan on it. [*The* SERVANT BOY *places the pan on the stones.*] Now take the ladle and fetch some sea-water. [*The* SERVANT BOY *ladles out water.*] When the pan is full put the gold coin in. Keep the fire burning, it must be a good fire to make the water boil quickly.

SERVANT BOY: Why didn't you say so before? I could easily have brought with me the rush-leaf fan that the woman's maid gave me. What am I going to fan the fire with? [*The* SERVANT BOY *fans the fire with his coat sleeve.*] Look, the water is boiling.

CHANG YÜ: The water's boiling! Let me look what's happening to the sea. [CHANG YÜ *looks in surprise.*] Extraordinary! It's true, the whole sea is bubbling and boiling, seething and steaming. The magic works!

SERVANT BOY: When the water boils here, the water in the sea boils too. How can it be that the sea does the same as the water in the pan?

Enter the ABBOT *in a panic.*

ABBOT: While I was meditating on my couch the Dragon King of the Eastern Sea sent someone to tell me that a young man had set the sea boiling, he didn't know how! The Dragon King is at his wits' end and doesn't know where to hide himself. He has begged me to persuade the youth to stop the fire at once. Why, it's none other than the student who came yesterday and took a room in my temple, the master scholar Chang Yü. My Temple of the Stone Buddha is close by the Eastern Sea. Now the Dragon is in danger, how can I stand by and do nothing to save him!

I see bloody vapour from the Palace of Crystals
 pouring to the sky,
I cannot breathe for the parching smoke that chokes
 my nose and mouth.
I do not know what tricks he employs,
He merely wishes to show off his power.
Even if there were thunder and rain,
Not even that would relieve the alarm.

See the brocade-scaled fish leap and pierce the hearts of waves,
And the silver-footed crabs scramble sideways up the shore to hide.

The ABBOT *approaches* CHANG YÜ.

You, master scholar, what are you boiling here?

CHANG YÜ: I am boiling the sea.

ABBOT: Why?

CHANG YÜ: I will tell you, your reverence. Last night while I was playing the *ch'in* in the temple a young woman came to listen. Later she told me she was the third daughter of a certain Mr Dragon and her name was Ch'iung-lien, and she promised to meet me on the day of the Mid-autumn Festival. I don't see her coming so I am boiling the sea here, and I am determined to boil it until she comes out.

ABBOT:

The student is unable to enjoy his love,
So he turns the sea into a scented bath!
A scholar should be gentle and gracious in his ways,
And practise the arts of peace and courtesy.
How can you resort to such a hot-headed trick?

CHANG YÜ: Don't interfere, your reverence. Go and beg your alms elsewhere.

ABBOT:

I do not come to beg for alms,
Nor do I seek your charity.
I come only to visit you.

CHANG YÜ: Visit me? I am a poor student, I have nothing to give.

ABBOT:

I am after all a Buddhist priest,
I do no wrong if I beg for alms.

CHANG YÜ: If I could find that woman and be accepted as a son-in-law, then I would have something to give you.

ABBOT:

Merely because of a beautiful girl
Not making a son-in-law of a fine fellow like you,
You call down this calamity from Heaven!
If you are poor, be poor!
And don't match yourself against her illustrious family.
Where did you get this boiling lead, this mercury and volcanic fire?
Where did you find this remedy for lovesickness?

CHANG YÜ: I shall be plain with your reverence. As long as the girl who came to me last night does not come out I shall go on boiling the sea.

ABBOT: Master scholar, listen to me! The Divine Dragon King of the Eastern Sea has appointed me his matchmaker to come and make you his son-in-law. What do you say to that?

CHANG YÜ: Don't make fun of me, your reverence. Look at the sea, one huge expanse of misty water. I am only a mortal, how am I to enter that?

SERVANT BOY: Don't worry, master. Simply follow the abbot. If he doesn't get drowned it's not likely that you will!

ABBOT [*aside*]:

I am very anxious to get to the bottom of this.
Take your time and consider well.

Point your finger at the water and it will turn to land,
Divide it and it will become firm beneath your feet,
As firm as if it were a path among the wild grass of
the plain.

CHANG YÜ: Won't it be dark going to the bottom of the sea?

ABBOT:

On the contrary, as bright as the sun coming out of his
mansion.

CHANG YÜ: No matter what you say, I am still only a mortal. How dare I go into the sea?

ABBOT:

Though the great sea is named the Eastern Ocean,
You are not to stand on ceremony.
Go! the Dragon King waits to receive you as his son-in-law.

CHANG YÜ: I've heard that the fairy Isle of Phoenixes and Unicorns in the middle of the Western Sea is surrounded by a ring of thin water three thousand feet deep where even a feather would sink. How then am I to go?

ABBOT:

Say nothing of rings of thin water three thousand feet
deep.
This is a land of shimmering brocade, a watery kingdom
of abundant riches.

CHANG YÜ *looks about.*

CHANG YÜ: The ocean seems so vast to me. It has no edge, no shore. It looks just as if it is joined to the sky. How terrifying!

ABBOT:

> You say it seems as vast and boundless as the sky;
> The more it shows how boundless is his magnanimity.

CHANG YÜ: Well, let me pack up my treasures. If only your reverence could ensure my affair were a success!

SERVANT BOY: That woman has a maid with her and she better be mine, otherwise I'll go on burning this fire!

ABBOT:

> Come, away, away!
> To orchid pavilions
> And painted halls.
> Believe me, believe me,
> Not a word I say
> Shall prove a lie.

CHANG YÜ: You are sure?

ABBOT:

> You,
> Your thoughts are always petty and mean.
> She,
> Already she is richly dressed and adorned,
> Soon,
> Soon to be married to you.
> Come, away, away!
> To the sleep of lovebirds beneath a golden net.

CHANG YÜ: I shall follow your reverence. If only we could come together soon like the moon at its full, and not break the promises we made!

ABBOT:

> You, beauty and her scholar, are so intent on love
> You have thrown her parents into consternation.

You with your handsome bearing and noble talents,
She with her jadelike body and flowerlike scents,
Both of you of one heart and mind,
Yours is a fitting marriage –
A husband and wife beyond compare!

Let us go. *Exeunt the* ABBOT *and* CHANG YÜ.

SERVANT BOY: My master has hurried off quite happily into the sea with his reverence and left me alone on the shore to look after these blessed treasures. If he really gets married I suppose it'll be a month before he comes out. I'll pack up all these things and go straight back to the temple, and see if I can't find the runner and have some fun with him. *Exit.*

ACT FOUR

Enter the DRAGON KING *and his* SEA-WARRIORS.

DRAGON KING: Ask the student and my daughter to come here.

Enter CHANG YÜ *and* CH'IUNG-LIEN.

CH'IUNG-LIEN: Go into the hall and meet my father.
CHANG YÜ: I am ready.
CH'IUNG-LIEN: When we bid each other good-bye that night, who would have thought we should see such a day!

Waves and billows stood between us, making strangers of friends.
I was afraid that in endless darkness we would each take separate ways.
I suffered in a living hell,
I tried hard to endure it all,

That from the farthest corners of the sea and sky
One day again we may be brought together.

CHANG YÜ *and* CH'IUNG-LIEN *make obeisance to the* DRAGON KING.

DRAGON KING: Where did the two of you meet?
CH'IUNG-LIEN:

I took advantage of a green sea and clear ripples,
A pleasant hour and lovely scene,
A light cloud and a slender mist,
A cool air encircling the crystal jar,
The jade dews trickling,
The gold wind rustling,
The season of the Mid-autumn Festival,
The time when all was solitude,
All voices hushed, the first watch of the night.

DRAGON KING: You had never met the student before! And it was the first watch and all was quiet! How did it happen that you promised to marry him? Tell me.
CH'IUNG-LIEN:

I went to him by the moon's brightness, mounting the steps,
Listening to the *ch'in*, a music out of this world,
Just like the call of a crane beyond the clouds,
Wild geese chanting at the edge of the sky,
The song of a bird on the branch of a tree.
He was longing to find a bride,
And I fearing to be left a maid.
Who could say if it were wise or foolish
Whether we chose to be lovers or not:

At once our thoughts and hearts were one,
Before we knew we were like fish in stream.

DRAGON KING: Who gave you those magic treasures, master scholar?

CHANG YÜ: I am a poor student. I couldn't hope to own any such treasures myself. But when I was in pursuit of your daughter I came to the seashore and there I chanced to meet a priestess, an immortal. She gave them to me.

DRAGON KING: You nearly burnt me to death, master scholar. I suppose my daughter is the cause of all this.

Enter TUNG HUA.

TUNG HUA: Listen to my command, Divine Dragon.

The DRAGON KING, CHANG YÜ *and* CH'IUNG-LIEN *fall to their knees.*

TUNG HUA: Chang Yü is not your son-in-law, Divine Dragon, nor is Ch'iung-lien your daughter. In their former lives they were a Gold Page and Jade Maiden living in the World of Immortals. Because there they fell in love with each other they were sent down to the lower world as a punishment. Now they have repaid their debt of love I have come to summon them from your watery kingdom to return again to the Jasper Pool and become immortal once more.

CH'IUNG-LIEN:

Together hand in hand today we mount to Heaven again,
This handkerchief as a pledge of love has not been kept in vain.

Idly we shall watch the Peaches of Immortality redden
on the trees,
For we have cast off this World of Dust and its
Boundless Bitter Sea.

AUTUMN IN HAN PALACE

by
Ma Chih-yüan
(*1250?–1320?*)

AUTUMN IN HAN PALACE

CHARACTERS

EMPEROR HUHANYA
MAO YEN-SHOU, *a counsellor*
EMPEROR YÜAN
WANG CHAO-CHÜN, *the Imperial Concubine Ming*
WU-LU CH'UNG-TSUNG, *the prime minister*
SHIH HSIEN, *a eunuch*
ENVOY TO EMPEROR HUHANYA
YOUNG EUNUCH, *attendant on Emperor Yüan*

CIVIL *and* MILITARY OFFICIALS, EUNUCHS
and SERVING MAIDS

AUTUMN IN HAN PALACE

THE WEDGE

Enter EMPEROR HUHANYA *with his* TRIBESMEN.

EMPEROR HUHANYA:

> The autumn wind strays in the ancient grass by my tent,
> The night moon wakes to the flute's lament.
> Chieftain of a million archers I am,
> My land a protectorate of the House of Han.

I am the Emperor Huhanya. My ancestors have long lived in the desert ruling unchallenged all the land in the north. Hunting is our livelihood, fighting our occupation. To escape us the Emperor Wên fled to the east; for fear of us Wei Chiang of the Kingdom of Tsin sued for peace. When the kingdoms of Ch'in and Han were at war and engaged in battle on the Central Plain our country became a very powerful nation. My grandfather Mao-tun laid siege for seven days to Emperor Kao of Han in Pai-têng. Peace between the two nations was only restored by means of a plan of Lou Ching's, laying down the condition that the princess royal be given in marriage to our emperor. Ever since the days of Emperor Hui and Empress Lü this has been the practice. During the reign of Emperor Hsüan there were endless quarrels among us brothers and the power of our nation declined. Now the tribes have elected me their Emperor. In fact I am a distant nephew of the House of Han. Recently I sent an envoy to offer tribute and demand the hand of the princess royal in marriage. I don't know whether or not the Emperor of Han will be prepared to honour the treaty. What a fine day it is! Let us be off into the desert to hunt!

Exeunt.

Enter MAO YEN-SHOU.

MAO YEN-SHOU:

I'm a man of a hawk's heart and a vulture's claw,
My business swindling the great and oppressing the poor.
All through flattery, cunning, treachery and greed,
I've got riches that one life is too short to exceed.

I am none other than Mao Yen-shou. I serve the court of Han as a counsellor of the middle rank. Because I've made it my one aim in life to flatter His Majesty with a hundred and one tricks, I've made the old boy very pleased. Whatever I say he listens to; whatever I propose he does. There isn't a single person inside or outside the court who doesn't respect me and fear me. And there is one trick in particular I've learned: only let the Emperor see as little of his ministers and as much of his women as possible and the favour he shows me will be secure. Here comes the Emperor, and I hadn't half finished what I wanted to say.

Enter EMPEROR YÜAN, *followed by* EUNUCHS *and* SERVING MAIDS.

EMPEROR YÜAN:

Ten reigns since Liu the fire-hearted held the throne,
The four hundred counties of the world I rule alone.
Treaties long have kept our frontiers at peace.
Henceforth on lofty pillows I can rest at ease.

I am Emperor Yüan of the House of Han. Since I came to the throne there has been peace throughout the length and breadth of my kingdom. It is not for any virtue on my part; the credit for maintaining it must go to my officials, both civil and military. After the death of my father all the women were released from the palace. Now the Inner Palace is a lonely place. What am I to do?

MAO YEN-SHOU: Your Majesty, even a peasant who raises an extra ten pecks of wheat from his harvest thinks of exchanging it for a wife. Your Majesty is not only the illustrious Son of Heaven, your riches include all within the bounds of the Four Seas. Why doesn't Your Majesty send officials travelling through the kingdom to select young women from every kind of family, be it prince's, duke's, prime minister's, soldier's or commoner's, as long as they are above fifteen and not over twenty and of good and proper appearance, and take these to fill your Inner Palace? What could be better than that?

EMPEROR YÜAN: What you've said is right. I appoint you our Selector, and with our royal decree you shall travel the whole of the kingdom to find and select these young women. Have a portrait painted of each you select and send them to me. Then according to the portraits I shall choose those I shall favour. When you return successful from your mission I shall see you are properly rewarded.

Exeunt.

ACT ONE

Enter MAO YEN-SHOU

MAO YEN-SHOU:

I grab any amount of gold that I please,
No fear of bloodbaths or royal decrees.
I want money in this life and nothing instead,
Who cares how they spit and curse once I am dead.

With the royal decree behind me I have travelled the length and breadth of the kingdom searching out young girls and selecting those for the Emperor. I've already chosen ninety-nine. Each family has exhausted itself giving me gifts. The gold and silver I've received is already something considerable. The other day I arrived at Tzŭ-kuai in Ch'êng-tu and selected one girl there, the daughter of a certain Wang, named Chao-chün. Her looks are quite dazzling; she is the most beautiful woman. Indeed there is not another her equal throughout the whole kingdom. However, her father is a mere farmer and he hasn't got much money. I asked him for a hundred taels of gold for placing her at the top of the list. He refused point blank, saying that for one thing he was poor and for another her looks were certain to surpass all the others. I am tempted to turn her down flat. [*thinks*] If I turn her down she will be even better off. I have it! It only needs a couple of lines to spoil this beauty's portrait. When she arrives at the capital she is certain to be dismissed to the chambers of the rejected. In this way she will suffer for the rest of her life. As the common saying goes, 'No gentleman only hates a little, no real man is without his spite.' *Exit.*

Enter WANG CHAO-CHÜN, *accompanied by two* SERVING MAIDS.

WANG CHAO-CHÜN:

One day I was summoned to Shang Yang Palace,
Ten years I have not seen the Emperor's face.
Who will keep me company this fine lonely night?
Shall only my *p'i pa* put my anxious thoughts to flight?

I am Wang Chao-chün. When I was eighteen I was chosen by His Majesty's grace to enter the Inner Palace. We did not think when His Majesty's Selector Mao Yen-shou demanded money and we refused that he would have my portrait altered for the worse. The Emperor has never seen me, and now I live here unnoticed in the Eternal Lane. When I was at home I was taught to play stringed and wind instruments quite well, and I learnt several tunes for the *p'i pa*. The night is deep and my heart is lonely. Let me play a tune to while away my cares. [*plays*]

Enter EMPEROR YÜAN, *followed by a* YOUNG EUNUCH *holding a lantern.*

EMPEROR YÜAN: Since the selection of women to fill the Inner Palace there are many I have not yet visited. They must complain bitterly awaiting my coming. Today I have had a thousand matters to attend to, and now I am taking advantage of a moment's leisure to walk about the palace grounds. Let us see who is destined to meet us.

I think they will not dare to lower their screens of pearls
For looking at Chao Yang Palace, each step a heaven away,

Troubled a little at bamboo shadows stirring in no wind,
Hating a little the moonlight shed on the window gauze,
Amid the sounds of strings and flutes hearing the royal carriage pass,
Like Herdboy on the Starry Shore awaiting the Spinning Maid's raft.[1]

Is that the sound of the *p'i pa* being played somewhere?

YOUNG EUNUCH: Yes, Your Majesty.

EMPEROR YÜAN:

Who is playing this secret melody
And pouring out her sorrows thus?

YOUNG EUNUCH: Quick, someone announce that the Emperor waits to be received!

EMPEROR YÜAN: Wait!

Do not bear word to her too hastily.
I fear that such a sudden favour
May startle her timorous heart.

Boy, go and see which palace lady is playing the *p'i pa*? Summon her to appear and receive us. But do not alarm her.

YOUNG EUNUCH: Who is the lady playing the *p'i pa*? His Majesty has come. Make haste and bid him welcome.

WANG CHAO-CHÜN *hastens forward.*

EMPEROR YÜAN:

Do not think you have done some wrong.
I wanted only myself to ask
To whom this place belonged?
Do not blame me that I have not come before.

Now I come to recompense the tears that wet your handkerchief,
To warm the shoes drenched soft-stepping in chilly dews.
Was it not Heaven that gave birth to such beauty?
It is fitting I should favour her.
Tonight beneath the decorated candles on their silver stems
The swelling petals spoke plainly of good news.

Boy, see how the light in the gauze lantern burns brighter. Lift it up higher so I may see.

Even the candle is roused to a radiance that streams through the red gauze.
Look –
My love!
Even her slender shadow too beautiful to bear!

WANG CHAO-CHÜN: If your humble servant had known earlier that Your Majesty was coming she would have come further to welcome Your Majesty. She has not welcomed Your Majesty early enough and deserves to die.

EMPEROR YÜAN:

At once she greets me with 'your humble servant',
Calls me again and again 'Your Majesty'.
Certainly she cannot come of simple birth.

Look, how perfect she is in every feature! What a beautiful woman!

Eyebrows drawn like two leaves in the palace style,
Hair well combed to frame her powdered face,
Fragrant temples decked with gold green flowers.

One smile from her could make a city fall.
If Prince Kou-chien had seen her on the Terrace at
  Ku-su,
He would have had none of Hsi Shih's wiles
And lost his throne and family ten years before.

With your extraordinary beauty, whose daughter can you be?

WANG CHAO-CHÜN: Your humble servant's name is Wang Chao-chün of Tzŭ-kuei in Ch'êng-tu. My father is the elder Wang. Since my grandfather's time we have been farmers. We are simple people and ignorant of the ways of the Royal Household.

EMPEROR YÜAN:

To see your eyebrows swept with black,
Your hair at your temples heaped raven-like,
Your waist as playful as the willow,
Your face the hue of clouds at dawn,
Not even Chao Yang Palace could hold a place for you.
Who would have you live by plough and hoe?
The Emperor's couch shall be reserved for you.
It is Heaven sends rain and dew to enrich the mulberry
  and hemp.
How else among ten thousand miles of hills and
  streams,
Should I have found you on one poor farm?

Why was your beauty not brought to my notice before?

WANG CHAO-CHÜN: When I was chosen Your Majesty's Selector Mao Yen-shou demanded gold. But we are a poor family and there was no way we could obtain such a sum, so he added several lines to spoil the eyes in my portrait. Because of this I was sent to the chambers of the rejected.

EMPEROR YÜAN: Boy, bring me the portrait and let me see.

The YOUNG EUNUCH *shows the portrait.*

There is only one question I shall ask the painter,
How could his colours have failed him so?
He draws the autumn ripple of your eye as if it were a flaw in jade,
As if indeed your eye were blind,
Or he were blind in both.
If the eight hundred beauties of my court were gathered to compare,
Not one could surpass my lady's portrait even with its flaw.

Boy, bear my orders to the captain of the palace guard to have Mao Yen-shou arrested and beheaded. Then report to me.

WANG CHAO-CHÜN: Your Majesty, the names of my parents in Ch'êng-tu are registered in the Book of Commoners. I hope Your Majesty in your grace and generosity will grant them some exemption and bestow on them a little honour.

EMPEROR YÜAN: Nothing could be easier.

At morning you gathered vegetables,
At night guarded melons,
In spring planted seeds for crops,
In summer watered hemp.
You seek to exempt your family from tithes and taxes on the court-house wall.
Now riches and honour will be yours when you pass through Chêng Yang Gate.
My position is as high as village elder's,

My house as large as country magistrate's.
I give thanks to Heaven and Earth
For taking pity on this poor son-in-law.
Who will dare again to oppress my father-in-law's house?

Approach and hear our royal decree. I name you the Imperial Concubine Ming.

WANG CHAO-CHÜN: How shall I be worthy of Your Majesty's favour!

WANG CHAO-CHÜN *kowtows to* EMPEROR YÜAN.

EMPEROR YÜAN:

Now let us exhaust this night with love,
And say no word of the morrow.

WANG CHAO-CHÜN: Tomorrow Your Majesty must come very early. I shall be here waiting for Your Majesty.

EMPEROR YÜAN: Tomorrow! Most likely I shall be lying in drunken sleep on the royal couch in Chao Yang Palace.

WANG CHAO-CHÜN: I am of poor and humble birth. Though I have found favour in Your Majesty's eyes I dare not hope to share the royal couch.

EMPEROR YÜAN:

Do not be troubled.
Tomorrow night at the Pavilion of the Western Palace,
Come quietly to receive me,
Or all the women of the palace I fear will start to play the *p'i pa*.

Exeunt EMPEROR YÜAN *and the* YOUNG EUNUCH.

WANG CHAO-CHÜN: His Majesty has gone. Close the gates now. I shall go to bed. *Exeunt.*

ACT TWO

Enter EMPEROR HUHANYA *with his* TRIBESMEN.

EMPEROR HUHANYA: Not long ago I sent an envoy to the kingdom of Han demanding the hand of the princess royal. The Emperor has refused, claiming that the princess is too young. I take it very ill! When I think of the countless women in the palaces of the House of Han, it would be no loss to him to send me one. Instead he sent my envoy straight back without more ado. I have considered raising an army and invading the south, but I fear it will put an end to the good relations of many years' standing between us. I shall see how matters proceed and then decide what seems best.

Enter MAO YEN-SHOU.

MAO YEN-SHOU: Who would have expected that the Emperor would one day go in person to visit Wang Chao-chün and there discover the truth. Now he intends to have me beheaded, but I took my opportunity and made my escape. There is nowhere I can go. Well, there's nothing left for it but to take this portrait of the beautiful Wang Chao-chün and present it to Emperor Huhanya. I'll persuade him to ask expressly for the woman in the painting. There's no fear the court of Han will refuse to give her up. I have been walking many days. At last I have arrived. I see a vast company of men and horses in the distance. Those must be their tents. Officer! Inform the Emperor Huhanya that a minister from the court of Han wishes to be received.

A SOLDIER *reports.*

EMPEROR HUHANYA: Ask him to come in. [*sees him*] Who are you?

MAO YEN-SHOU: I am Mao Yen-shou, an official of the middle rank in the court of Han. In the Pavilion of the Western Palace in our kingdom of Han we have a woman of great beauty, named Wang Chao-chün. Her beauty is unsurpassed. When Your Majesty sent an envoy to ask for the hand of the princess royal, Wang Chao-chün asked to be sent instead. But the Master of Han could not bring himself to part with her and would not let her go. I repeatedly remonstrated with His Majesty saying that for the sake of a woman how could he destroy the good relations between two nations. For all that he plans to have me killed. So I have brought a portrait of this beautiful woman and offer it to Your Majesty. Your Majesty could send an envoy expressly to demand the woman in the painting. You would be certain to obtain her. This is her portrait.

MAO YEN-SHOU *comes forward with the painting;* EMPEROR HUHANYA *looks at it.*

EMPEROR HUHANYA: How in the world can there exist such a woman! If I could make her my queen, there'd be nothing else I could wish for. I shall send an envoy at once to the Emperor of Han with a letter demanding the hand of Wang Chao-chün in marriage. If he refuses I shall send an army southwards without delay and he will be hard put to it to defend his kingdom. *Exeunt.*

Enter WANG CHAO-CHÜN *with her* SERVING MAIDS.

WANG CHAO-CHÜN: Since the day I gained the Emperor's favour a month or more has suddenly gone by. His Majesty is so much in love with me he has long been absent from his court. Today, I hear he has gone to hold an audience, so I shall go to my dressing-table and see to my make-up. Then if His Majesty should come I shall be ready to wait upon him. [*looks into a mirror*]

Enter EMPEROR YÜAN.

EMPEROR YÜAN: Since I met Wang Chao-chün in the Pavilion of the Western Palace I feel as though I were drunk, as though I had lost my wits. For a long time I have been absent from the court. Today I held an audience but I could not even wait for it to end. I must go again to the Western Palace to look at her once more.

Each season its measure of rain and dew,
A kingdom rich in hills and streams,
Officials loyal and well-employed,
No cares to unsettle happy sleep.
I worship one of snow-white teeth and eyes like stars,
The wasteful daytime I can hardly bear!
Some sickness now has overtaken me,
Part anxious for my realm and people,
Part languishing for love and wine.
How can I bear her heavenly fragrance lingering on my
 dragon-robe sleeves!
Everything that is hers is lovely,
In everything our thoughts are one.
To while away the lonely mortal hours
She accompanies me to roam at leisure,
Happiest when we climb the tower by pear trees
 blossoming in the moon
Or play at guessing games beneath the lotus lamp,
Her form twenty years shaped in tenderness,
Our marriage destined for five hundred years.
Her face tells a thousand endless tales of charm.

Like the Goddess of Mercy without her sacred willow,
One look at her ensures long life.
How shall it end, the love that binds our hearts,
But in the moment rains cease and clouds depart.

[*sees her*]

I will not frighten her. I'll look on quietly.

Within the Long Gate Palace my former concubines complain.
How could they know in the Western Palace I dwell among my dreams?
I love to see her at her evening make-up,
The shading not quite right,
A line not quite perfect,
And she stays before the mirror self-ashamed.

EMPEROR YÜAN *goes up behind* WANG CHAO-CHÜN, *looking on.*

Here where I stand behind her dressing-table
Behold! Ch'ang Ngo in the Hall of Immense Cold
Caught in a moon's brightness.

WANG CHAO-CHÜN *sees* EMPEROR YÜAN; *enter* WU-LU CH'UNG-TSUNG, *the prime minister, and* SHIH HSIEN, *a eunuch.*

PRIME MINISTER: I am Wu-lu Ch'ung-tsung, Prime Minister to His Majesty. This is Shih Hsien, a eunuch. After the audience today there arrived an envoy from Emperor Huhanya demanding the hand of Wang Chao-chün in marriage. I shall have to report to the Emperor. Here I am at the Pavilion of the Western Palace. I'll go straight in. [*sees the* EMPEROR] I beg to inform Your Majesty that

Emperor Huhanya of the North has sent an envoy saying that Mao Yen-shou has taken a portrait of Wang Chao-chün and presented it to his master. His master now demands the hand of Wang Chao-chün in marriage as a condition of keeping the peace between our two nations. If he is refused, he will send a great army southwards and we will find our kingdom overrun.

EMPEROR YÜAN: We maintain our troops for thousands of days to have them ready for just such a day as this. Is our court full of officers and officials for nothing? Who will defeat these foreign troops for us? Are you all afraid of swords and arrows? Can you not exert yourselves? How can you ask Lady Wang to go to appease a foreign emperor?

> In every age nations rise and fall,
> Shields and spears are never laid aside.
> You take your living from the Emperor,
> Are your lives not the Emperor's to command?
> In times of peace
> You make boast of your achievements.
> When a crisis threatens
> You would exile my love.
> Is it for nothing you take your wages from the royal house?
> Will you not share in banishing your Emperor's sorrows?
> But there you chain yourselves to trees afraid to sprain your wrists,
> And here you hold tight to railings afraid to break your necks!

PRIME MINISTER: The Emperor Huhanya says that because of your infatuation with Wang Chao-chün Your Majesty has completely neglected the duties of an emperor and endangered the safety of your country. If you do not surrender her he will raise a punitive force and invade our land. As I remember, the tyrant Chou lived only for the favours of his concubine Ta I and his kingdom was conquered and he himself killed. That should be a warning.

EMPEROR YÜAN:

But I have built no tower cloud-high to pluck down stars.
You sleep beneath thick quilts,
Eat from rows of tripods,
Ride lusty horses,
Dress in light furs.
You must have seen her slender waist dancing like willow in spring wind,
How can you let her pendants' shadow shiver in moonlight on a green mound,
Or the music of her *p'i pa* fade at autumn by Black Dragon River?

PRIME MINISTER: Your Majesty, our country has neither well-trained soldiers nor generals brave enough to fight. If some blunder were committed, what should we do? I hope Your Majesty will sever your affections and surrender Wang Chao-chün. It will save the lives of thousands of our people.

EMPEROR YÜAN:

On that day long ago who showed himself the hero,
Displayed his rival Hsiang Yu's head
And delivered this land over to Liu the fire-hearted?
All was the work of General Han at the battle of Nine Mile Mountain.

And the achievement of his ten great feats of arms.
You too serve the court of Han,
But your golden seals and purple cords you wear in vain.
You too live within crimson gates
And favour singing robes and dancing sleeves,
But when the frontier is breached your courage fails,
And when your homes are threatened you turn tail.
Like geese with arrows stuck through their bills,
Not one of you dares to cough!
I suffer torments for her.
She is still young, so young,
And there is none to save her.
What blood of yours is on her hands to earn her such revenge?
Enough, enough –
It would not surprise me if the whole court were Mao Yen-shou's.
I,
In vain do I command three thousand companies of troops,
The four hundred counties of the Middle Plain,
I can only wait to sue for peace.
How easy it is to raise a thousand men,
How hard to find one man to lead them.

SHIH HSIEN: The foreign envoy waits outside to be received, Your Majesty.

EMPEROR YÜAN: So be it! Send him in.

Enter the FOREIGN ENVOY; *he sees* EMPEROR YÜAN.

FOREIGN ENVOY: The Emperor Huhanya has sent me to remind Your Majesty, Emperor of the Great House of Han, that our country in the north and Your Majesty's country in the south have long lived at peace by virtue of the marriages that unite us. Envoys have twice been sent to ask for the hand of the princess royal in marriage and have been refused. Now Mao Yen-shou has presented our Emperor with the portrait of a certain beautiful woman. His Majesty has sent me especially to request that Wang Chao-chün be made our queen. Only in this way can peace be maintained between our two nations. If Your Majesty refuses to comply we have an army a million strong. It can be ordered at any time to advance southwards and determine the issue by war. It is earnestly hoped that your sacred decision will not be wrong.

EMPEROR YÜAN: For the present conduct the envoy to the official residence for him to rest. [*Exit the* FOREIGN ENVOY.] You, ministers and generals, consult together! Present us with some plan for holding the foreign troops at bay and saving Wang Chao-chün from being sent to appease their emperor. But doubtless you will take advantage of Lady Wang's good and tender nature. In the days when Empress Lü was on the throne whatever she said none dared to disobey. If this is to be the situation, we shall soon have no need for ministers and generals; we shall be dependent entirely on beautiful women to bring peace and order to the nation.

All you can do, you ministers and generals,
Is shake the mountains with 'Long live the Emperor',
Dance attendance and raise only dust.
From now on
Let there be no more warlike deeds,
We shall do battle between the sheets.

WANG CHAO-CHÜN: I have already received great favours from Your Majesty. I would gladly sacrifice my life to repay you. I am willing to go to appease the foreign emperor if war may be averted and my name recorded for generations to come. But our love, how am I to part with that?

EMPEROR YÜAN: And I too, how am I to part with you?

PRIME MINISTER: Your Majesty, sever your affections and renounce your love. Think first of the good of your nation, and lose no time in sending Lady Wang away.

EMPEROR YÜAN:

Today she shall marry the foreign emperor.
Prime minister, you need not distress yourself further.
My love is fated to have a country to which she cannot return.
Where she goes no golden clouds rise from the peaks of green mountains.
When she comes there each from afar we shall gaze out,
Awaiting across autumn skies a wild goose promising news.
It is ordained that this year I bring sorrow on myself,
And Wang Chao-chün too, waste away with grief.
Her hat of emerald feathers
And fragrant silk ribbons
Abandoned for a warm hood of brocade
And pearls stitched to a coat of fur.

Escort Lady Wang to the official residence today and deliver her over to the foreign envoy. Then tomorrow we shall go ourself to see her off at Pa Ling Bridge and drink with her a farewell cup of wine.

PRIME MINISTER: That you must not do, Your Majesty. I'm

afraid you will make yourself the laughing-stock of the foreigners.

EMPEROR YÜAN: I have agreed to all your wishes, why can't you agree to mine? Whatever happens I shall see her off. Mao Yen-shou, a curse upon you!

How shall I prolong our first night's dream?
Henceforth I shall not see Chang-an[2] for looking at the northern stars,
Forced like Herdboy to lament his Spinning Maid upon a midnight shore.

PRIME MINISTER: It is not we who are forcing Lady Wang to go to appease the foreign emperor. What else can we do? The foreign envoy demanded her by name. There have been instances enough since ancient times of nations falling because of beautiful women.

EMPEROR YÜAN:

Though for such as Wang Chao-chün nations rise and fall,
Whose position is like mine – Emperor with no freedom!
How shall I lock away my purple-white horses,
The green sedan-chair and our fragrant carriage of former times?
Shall it be I who roll up the red curtains, fold back the embroidered quilt?
Who would dream that for itself alone the moon must shine and water flow?
So mournful thoughts run on and on!

WANG CHAO-CHÜN: Though it is for the good of the kingdom I go, I can hardly bear to leave Your Majesty.

EMPEROR YÜAN:

> When my lady is hungry take a little of their tasteless salt meat,
> When thirsty take a dipperful of their sour milk or gruel.
> Sad willow boughs I shall have to break,
> And drink a cup of farewell wine.
> Soon I shall see you hurried on your journey,
> In search of a lodging for the night.
> Then pain and anguish in your heart
> You will turn your gaze behind,
> No more to see I fear our phoenix halls and dragon towers.
> Tonight turn me towards Pa Ling Bridge to sleep!

Exeunt.

ACT THREE

Enter WANG CHAO-CHÜN *followed by the* FOREIGN ENVOY; *Hu music playing.*

WANG CHAO-CHÜN: The Emperor Huhanya has sent for me. If I do not go our kingdom will be lost. There is no choice but for me to be sent across the frontier to appease him. But to go to the land of Hu with its winds and frosts, how am I to endure it! How true the ancient saying is, 'An ill fate befalls all those born fair; the fault is not the world's but theirs.'

Enter EMPEROR YÜAN *followed by* OFFICIALS *and* EUNUCHS.

EMPEROR YÜAN: Today at Pa Ling Bridge I must bid my love farewell. Already I am there.

For brocade and sable robes she will shed her palace
clothes.
Soon only her image shall I have on which to gaze,
Bygone joys as short as gold bit,
New sorrows long as jade-handled whip.
We were lovebirds in golden halls,
Now our wings bear us apart
Who knows what will become of us?

You ministers and generals, consult together! Can you find no way of keeping back the foreign troops and saving Lady Wang from being surrendered to their emperor?

Ministers, consider –
Return the envoy with gifts and rich rewards,
It is my love and I that bear the grief.
Even the humblest traveller departs with two farewells.[3]
And now frail willows of Wei-ch'êng are joined to our
sorrow,
And bitter waters beneath Pa Ling Bridge add their
despair.
Only you officials refuse to let yourselves be moved.
Oh to think of the sorrow gathered that night in her
p'i pa!

EMPEROR YÜAN *dismounts from his horse and grieves with* WANG CHAO-CHÜN.

Attendants, sing the farewell song slowly, while Lady Wang and I drink a parting cup of wine.

Do not take this parting song too lightly.
So near to you is yet a world away.
Take up the jade goblet slowly, slowly.

Only let me draw out the hour with you.
Do not ask if there is discord in the tune,
If we can but prolong the song by half a phrase.

FOREIGN ENVOY: Lady, will you come with us now? It is already getting dark.

EMPEROR YÜAN:

Have pity! must I part so heavily
And you only think to hasten your return.
Already my heart has gone ahead of you to Li Ling's desert tower,
Only afterwards to turn again and think of her in dreams.

WANG CHAO-CHÜN: Now I am going away I do not know when I shall see Your Majesty again. I leave behind all my Han Palace clothes.

Today a woman of the Palace of Han,
Tomorrow a wife in the land of Hu.
How shall I endure a new master's robes,
To enhance my beauty for another?

WANG CHAO-CHÜN *lays aside her clothes.*

EMPEROR YÜAN:

Why leave behind your dancing robes
For the west wind to scatter their fragrance of old?
Truly I dread my royal carriage passing again Green Moss Lane,
Suddenly to come upon the Chamber of Sweet Scents,
And then to remember you before your mirror making up,
And your enchanting face –
And all at once a pang to strike my heart again.

Today I must see Wang Chao-chün cross our frontier,
When to return like General Su Wu[4] to her native land?

FOREIGN ENVOY: Come, madam, please. We have delayed long enough.

EMPEROR YÜAN: Very well, very well! Do not blame me for your going, Wang Chao-chün. [*takes his leave*] Who would have me called the Emperor of Great Han!

Have I become the tyrant of Ch'u bidding his favourite farewell?
Then where are my generals of the Jade Door Pass to fight my battles in the west?

PRIME MINISTER: Do not take this so to heart, Your Majesty.

EMPEROR YÜAN:

Where she goes are no seas of purple or golden beams.
For what purpose have we kept our men-at-arms!
Long before you raise your swords and spears
Your hearts are already leaping like young deer.

PRIME MINISTER: Let us go back to the Palace, Your Majesty.

EMPEROR YÜAN:

Prime minister, you who harmonize *yin* and *yang*,
Control the workings of the state,
Govern the nation, keep the king's peace,
Develop the land and open up frontiers,
If I, your Emperor,
Were to send away your favourite serving maid,
To turn her back on village well and leave behind her native soil

To lie in snow and sleep in frost,
If she does not yearn for spring winds and for painted halls
I shall create you a prince imperial.

PRIME MINISTER: Please don't detain her unreasonably, Your Majesty. Let her go on her way.

EMPEROR YÜAN:

What, a great emperor and not to love Wang Chao-chün!
Ah,
How am I to bear it when she parts and turns to look!
How bear to imagine the scattering wind and snow,
The pennants and banners of the envoy's train casting shadows afar,
The solemn music of drum and horn shaking the mountain paths.
Ah,
I gaze out upon this rugged wilderness heart-stricken.
The grass has already turned to yellow,
The colour already touched by frost,
The hounds have shed their coats of grey,
The hunters stand ready with tasselled spears,
The horses loaded with luggage,
The carts carrying food.
The chase begins in the Royal Hunting-Ground.
She, yes she
With breaking heart she bids her lord farewell.
I, yes I
I take her hand and go where we shall part.
She with her caravan moves off into the desert wilds,
in my royal carriage return to Hsien-yang,

Return to Hsien-yang
Past palace walls,
Past palace walls
Round winding galleries,
Round winding galleries
Near the fragrant chamber,
Near the fragrant chamber
The moon misty yellow,
The moon misty yellow
And the night air chill,
The night air chill
And cold cicadas weep,
Cold cicadas weep
At green gauze windows,
Green gauze windows!
Let me not think –
Oh,
Not to think
Is for a heart of iron!
A heart of iron
Would still let fall a thousand sad streams of tears.
Tonight my lady's portrait shall hang in Chao Yang Palace,
And there I shall wait upon her,
Burning tall candles on silvery stems to light up her beautiful face.

PRIME MINISTER: Will you not return to your carriage, Your Majesty? Lady Wang is already far away.

EMPEROR YÜAN:

Though I might feign some pretext to my ministers,
I fear the tell-tale pen of chroniclers.

Oh, not to see her flowerlike spirit –
How shall it bear the harsh light of the steppes?
How often on their way has she stood still,
Hesitating,
Suddenly to hear the wild geese from the border flying south.
Ah! Ah! their cry sounds sonorous and deep,
And before her eyes only cattle and sheep,
The sound of the carriage with its sad burden creaking up the slope. *Exeunt.*

Enter EMPEROR HUHANYA *with his* TRIBESMEN *escorting* WANG CHAO-CHÜN.

EMPEROR HUHANYA: Today the Kingdom of Han has honoured our ancient treaty. The Emperor has sent me Wang Chao-chün to be my wife and to unite our two nations in peace. I have created her my Queen of the Peaceful North. So war between our two countries has been averted. All to the good! Send out the command, generals. Let us make our way northwards. [*They proceed.*]

WANG CHAO-CHÜN: What is this place?

FOREIGN ENVOY: This is Black Dragon River, the boundary between our land and the Kingdom of Han. All to the south belongs to the House of Han and all to the north to us.

WANG CHAO-CHÜN: Great king, may I ask for a cup of wine, to make a libation to the south and bid farewell to the Kingdom of Han before we start our long journey? [WANG CHAO-CHÜN *pours a libation.*] Emperor of Han, this life of mine is ended. I shall await you in the life to come.

WANG CHAO-CHÜN *throws herself into the river;* EMPEROR HUHANYA *in alarm goes to save her but fails.*

EMPEROR HUHANYA [*sighs*]: Alas, alas! Wang Chao-chün could not bear to enter our kingdom and has thrown herself into the river and drowned. So be it, so be it! Let us bury her here by the river bank and call her grave the Green Mound. Now she is dead, and we have brought enmity between the House of Han and ourselves to no purpose. It is all the scheming of that scoundrel Mao Yen-shou. Go, men! Arrest Mao Yen-shou and escort him back to the Kingdom of Han to be punished. Then the alliance between our two countries shall be restored as before, and our ties once again be those of true kinship. *Exeunt.*

ACT FOUR

Enter EMPEROR YÜAN *followed by* EUNUCHS.

EMPEROR YÜAN: Since Wang Chao-chün was sent away to become the Emperor Huhanya's wife a hundred days have passed and I have granted no audience. The night is lonely and I am sick at heart. I will hang up this portrait to comfort me a little.

A chillness rises in my royal palace,
The night is high, all quiet within the women's
  chambers,
Facing the Silver Terrace Gate the speck of one cold
  lamp.
To see the quilts and pillows
Where I lie down to sleep
Reminds me all the more of my unhappy fate.
Ten thousand miles from my dragon palace,
Tell me where does she rest tonight, my one true soul?

The incense in the censer is nearly burnt out, boy. Add a little more.

> Lady, you are like the Temple of the Bamboo Grove,
> Half seen you disappear,
> Leaving no more than your shadow behind.
> Until I die,
> As I shall live
> I shall do homage to you.

I feel tired suddenly. Let me sleep awhile.

> Dreams of lovers meeting,
> How hard they are to reach!
> Where are you, my love, my love?
> Why does your spirit not appear to me?
> Am I to be denied the one night's sweet dream
> allowed Prince Hsiang of Ch'u?

EMPEROR YÜAN *sleeps; enter* WANG CHAO-CHÜN.

WANG CHAO-CHÜN: I am Wang Chao-chün. I was sent to the north to appease a foreign emperor, but I have secretly escaped and returned. Is that not my lord? Your Majesty, I have come back.

Enter a FOREIGN SOLDIER.

FOREIGN SOLDIER: While I was dozing a moment, Wang Chao-chün stole away and came home. I hurried off after her, and here I am in Han Palace. Ah, Wang Chao-chün, there you are!

The FOREIGN SOLDIER *seizes* WANG CHAO-CHÜN *and leads her off;* EMPEROR YÜAN *awakes.*

EMPEROR YÜAN: I just saw Wang Chao-chün return. How is it I don't see her now?

A moment ago a soldier of Huhanya's was here,
Calling my Wang Chao-chün by name.
Yet when I called you by the lamp, lady, you gave me no answer –
But is it only your portrait I saw?
Suddenly I heard from Immortal Halls the sound of phoenix flutes
Playing no less than the Nine Variations of Shun.
Daylight brings me no sight of her,
Nor am I yet allowed one sleep till dawn
To be with her in one dream more.

A wild goose cries.

But listen – a wild goose crying over the Long Gate Palace.
How can it know there is one here so lonely?

It cries again.

It must be that its time is past,
And strength is spent,
Food and water scarce perhaps,
And bones and feathers grown light.
Should it go back
It dreads the wide nets of the south.
Should it go on
It fears the mighty northern bows.
Despairing it sounds as for Wang Chao-chün thinking of the Master of Han,
Mournful as the ancient dirge sung for the brave T'ien Hêng,[5]

Sad as the midnight songs of Ch'u[6] before the
destruction of Ch'in.

It cries again.

Confound it, the cries of this bundle of feathers only make me more sad!

Already I am sick at heart,
Now comes another enemy to torment me all the more,
Its cries now sometimes slow,
Now sometimes sharp –
Cold harmony with the watches of the night.

It cries again.

These are not the sounds my heart loves to hear,
Of orioles singing in woodland groves,
The cool splashing of a mountain stream.
I see only mountains and rivers reaching far and
Heaven like a mirror.
How am I to bear it more, this endless night on marble
steps
Loathing the moon's brightness!

YOUNG EUNUCH: Do not torment yourself, Your Majesty. Think more of your royal person.

EMPEROR YÜAN: I simply cannot help myself.

Do not say that I am easily moved,
You officials too can hate.
This was not swallows chattering in the painted eaves,
Nor orioles singing in the flowering trees.
Wang Chao-chün has left her homeland.
Who knows where in sorrow she may hear this too?

It cries again.

Ah! Ah! a flock of geese fly past the smartweed banks,
One goose alone leaves not the phoenix walls.
In painted eaves the iron horses ring and ring,
Within the palace the royal couch grows cold,
Cold these watches of the night,
Wind rustling in falling leaves,
The candle dim, the Long Gate Palace quiet.
A cry encircles the Palace of Han.
Another cry reaches to Wei-ch'êng.
White hairs steal upon me and my body fails.
There is no counsel that can make me well.

Enter the PRIME MINISTER.

PRIME MINISTER: Your Majesty, this morning after your audience an envoy came from Emperor Huhanya bringing back Mao Yen-shou in chains, saying that it was Mao Yen-shou's treachery that destroyed the friendship between our two nations and brought about this calamity. Wang Chao-chün is dead. It is his Emperor's wish that the old alliance between us be restored. The envoy humbly awaits Your Majesty's sacred decree.

EMPEROR YÜAN: Since it has come to this, have Mao Yen-shou beheaded and offer his head as a sacrifice to the spirit of Wang Chao-chün, our Imperial Concubine Ming. For the envoy and his retinue prepare a great feast, and reward him abundantly before he returns.

A STRATAGEM OF INTERLOCKING RINGS

Anonymous
(*early fourteenth century*)

A STRATAGEM OF INTERLOCKING RINGS

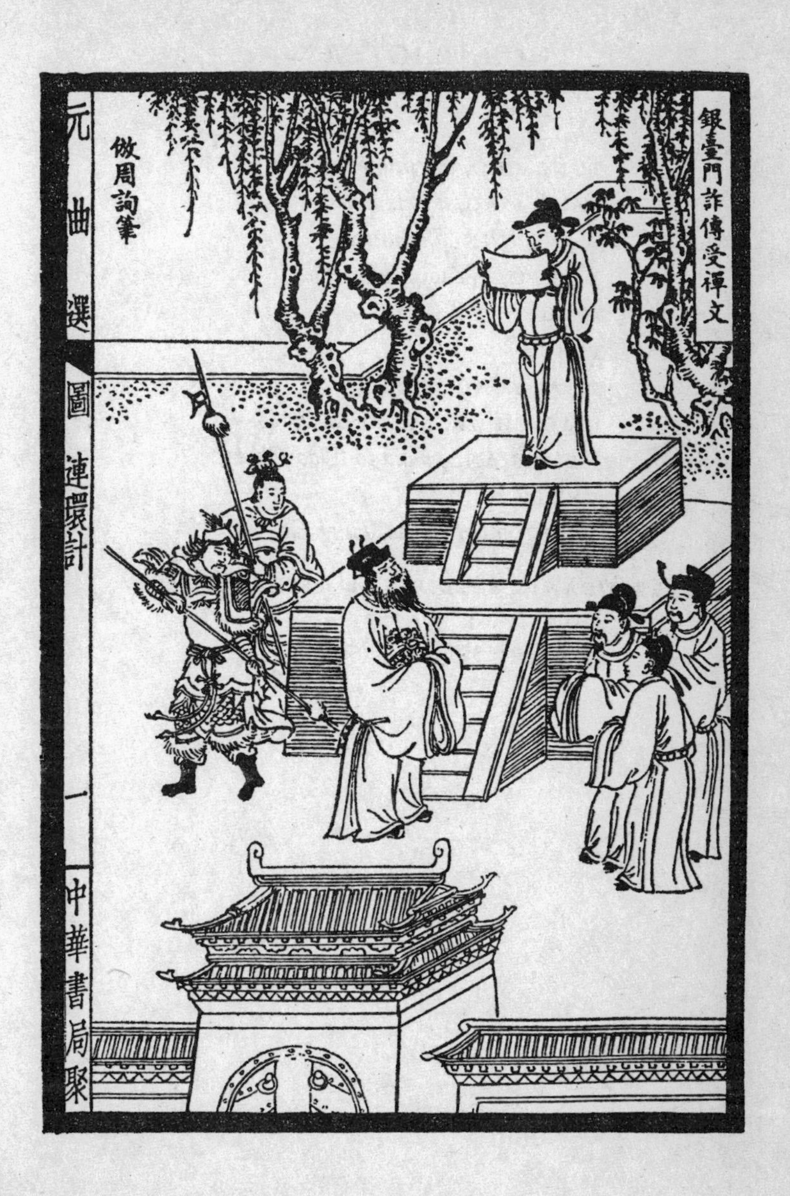

CHARACTERS

TUNG CHO, *the prime minister*
YANG PIAO, *a field marshal*
WANG YÜN, *a minister*
T'AI PO, *a Taoist immortal*
LI JU
LI SU
TS'AI YUNG
TIAO CH'AN, *wife to Lü Pu*
MEI-HSIANG, *maid to Tiao Ch'an*
CHI LÜ
LÜ PU, *foster son to Tung Cho*

ATTENDANTS, SOLDIERS *and a* SERVANT BOY

A STRATAGEM OF INTERLOCKING RINGS

ACT ONE

Enter TUNG CHO *followed by* LI JU *and* LI SU *and* SOLDIERS.

TUNG CHO: I am Tung Cho. I was made a general when still a young man, and have many frontier battles to my credit. Later I was recommended to serve in the palace because of the corruption of the Ten Eunuchs, and making my way up step by step I have now become prime minister. Whenever I go into the palace I let the sword at my waist show a little of its sharp blade; every one of the officials turns as white as a sheet! Moreover I've many extremely able counsellors and generals under me. These two for example – Li Ju and Li Su. Both braver than the bravest of men and wiser than the most wise. I have thousands of the finest horses and a hundred thousand valiant soldiers. I do as I please in the capital and hold the city of Chang-an in fear and trembling. I could be Master of Han at a flick of my wrist. There's only that fellow Wang Yün, full of treacherous tricks. All the time he watches me, and I have to be constantly on my guard. I have people following him wherever he goes, wherever he stays, wherever he sits, wherever he sleeps. The slightest move he makes is reported to me at once. Someone told me today that after leaving the palace Wang Yün did not go home but went straight to the house of Field Marshal Yang Piao. I'm afraid that the two of them might be hatching some sort of plot. I shall go directly to Yang Piao's house myself, and put an end to their scheming. *Exeunt.*

Enter YANG PIAO *with* ATTENDANTS.

YANG PIAO: I am Yang Piao. Emperor Hsien holds the throne but the prime minister Tung Cho has all the power. It is at his will that men live or die, that fortunes rise or fall. Not one of the hundreds of officials dares to look him in the face. His Majesty is dejected and helpless, he can do nothing. How true the saying is, 'When the emperor is helpless his ministers will be abused, and when the emperor is abused, his ministers will die.' If I do not share His Majesty's misfortunes, can I be called a loyal subject? I am waiting my chance to kill this arch-villain. But what can I do about Lü Pu, that house slave of his? There is no one his equal for bravery. I cannot see my way to doing it as yet. It seems there is only one person with whom I can work – Wang Yün. He is wise and resourceful. I've asked him to come and discuss matters. When the minister comes, report to me.

ATTENDANT: Yes, Your Excellency.

Enter WANG YÜN.

WANG YÜN: I am Wang Yün, a minister of the imperial court. Field Marshal Yang Piao has sent for me. I don't know what it's all about; I must go and see. But I feel ashamed, I am old and my powers are failing; there is nothing I can do in return for the Emperor's favours.

My springs and autumns it could be said I waste,
Forced for no reason to prolong my days, my nights.
For nothing am I given
Fine horses, light furs.
What burden is mine to become haggard and thin?
It is for this kingdom of the House of Han
That my brows are knit with sorrow for the court,

As when rain comes while flowers are still in bloom.
Why should leaves fall and autumn return out of time?
All officials at first are eager to outdo the other,
But will hang back in fright when asked for proof of their worth.
If I could enlist a person to put the kingdom to rights
I would not leave my name in vain to generations to come.

I've arrived at Yang Piao's gate. Will someone announce me?

ATTENDANT: The minister Wang Yün.

YANG PIAO: Please come in.

WANG YÜN: You sent for me, Field Marshal. What is it you wish to discuss?

YANG PIAO: It is more than four hundred years since the House of Han came to power. Not until the reign of His Majesty our Emperor Hsien has there been any period of its history when it was in danger of falling. The prime minister Tung Cho has all the power in his hands, and he persecutes all the other ministers and officials. There seems to be nothing one can do. I've run through the names of all the officials in the palace; for wisdom and resourcefulness there is not one your equal. I wonder if together we can't think out some efficient means for performing our duty to the state. What do you say? It was His Majesty's orders that I should send for you. What plan can you suggest for seizing Tung Cho?

WANG YÜN: Hush, Field Marshal. The wicked scoundrel is powerful and his influence is immense. It will not be so easy to get rid of him. He has ears and eyes everywhere. If news of our design leaks out, it will be courting disaster.

YANG PIAO: Even so, we have been servants of Han for generations, and we have vowed never to live side by side with such villainy. If there is something to be done, we will give our lives to achieve it. We've no need to fear him.

TUNG CHO *rushes in with* SOLDIERS.

TUNG CHO: I've come straight to Yang Piao's house, I shall unmask the old villain! Go and say that Prime Minister Tung Cho is at the gate.

An ATTENDANT *reports.*

ATTENDANT: Prime Minister Tung Cho has come, Your Excellency.

YANG PIAO [*alarmed*]: Just as you suspected! Prime Minister Tung Cho is here. We must go straight out and welcome him.

YANG PIAO *and* WANG YÜN *come out to welcome* TUNG CHO.

TUNG CHO: Ah, Minister Wang is also here. What are you two discussing?

YANG PIAO: After our work at court was over, Minister Wang and I just happened to come here to talk at more leisure, that is all. We haven't discussed anything.

TUNG CHO: When the two of you saw me approaching, Wang Yün, you both seemed to be frightened. You must be planning to get rid of me.

WANG YÜN: Our lives are in your hands, Prime Minister. How dare we?

TUNG CHO [*smiles*]: So you appreciate my power is something to be reckoned with.

WANG YÜN:

Count Lü Pu should have the command of the army.
We were discussing when to consult with him,
Waiting to find an auspicious day.

TUNG CHO: So you're waiting to find an auspicious day. Perhaps you're thinking of inviting me to a drinking party?

WANG YÜN: No, not that. We were looking for an early opportunity to invite the prime minister to mount the throne.

TUNG CHO [*smiles*]: I am afraid such a position will never be mine! But if ever that day should come, you shall be given whatever you ask.

WANG YÜN: [*aside*] You say we shall be given whatever we ask? I fear there are no bounds to your treacherous heart.

TUNG CHO: Let me ask you, Field Marshal Yang. Since the world began has there ever been an emperor willing to let another have his crown?

YANG PIAO: There's an old saying, 'The righteous shall conquer the unrighteous, the wicked shall give up their thrones to the good.'

TUNG CHO: In that case the logic of what you have proposed today is plain, Minister Wang.

WANG YÜN:

There was a certain Emperor Shun of Yü,
A man meek and dutiful who inherited the Kingdom
of T'ang.
There was another, the first Emperor of Ch'in,
A tyrant who overthrew the House of Chou and did
not live long.

Now comes another great emperor
Intending to usurp the throne, whose arrogance will only make him an object of scorn.

TUNG CHO: I've been racking my brains over this problem but it can't be done at one stroke, which infuriates me. So far as I can see there is no one more powerful than I inside or outside the palace. If I want to stage a takeover who is there who'll dare to oppose me? It would mean disaster for him straightaway. There'd be no saving his own life or his family's – not a single member of his nine generations would be spared.

WANG YÜN: I've been studying the stars at night. The days of the House of Han are numbered. Prime Minister, your noble deeds are there for everyone to see. The kingdom should be yours, and not the House of Han's. It is only a matter of time.

TUNG CHO [*smiles*]: Even if the heavenly portents say so, I'm only afraid that such good fortune isn't for me.

WANG YÜN: Didn't you know, Prime Minister, that inside the Gate of the Silver Terrace a great platform is being erected? If this is not for the enthronement, what else is it for?

TUNG CHO: If ever I succeed in this great scheme, those who are for me shall be my friends and those against me my enemies. This is something to be remembered, is it not?

WANG YÜN:

Admiration for your virtues will ensure it, not your power.
We pray your Dragon Stream will sweep away the filth of the world,

That your hand on your Dragon Sword will right the wrongs of the realm,
That seated in your Dragon Hall you hold the beauties of this land secure.

TUNG CHO: This calls for quick action and no more delay.

WANG YÜN:

Only be sure that you seek the goodwill of the people.
Where there is musk, there will fragrance be found.
One must not work against the dictates of Heaven.
Do nothing wrong and you will come to no harm.

TUNG CHO: The success of this depends entirely on the help you two ministers can give me. Believe me, I shall see you amply rewarded.

YANG PIAO: Rest assured, Prime Minister. It's only a matter of a few days. We'll select a day of good omen, then we shall all come and present Your Honour to the throne.

TUNG CHO: Since my arrival at court, I have had the army well in hand, millions of them. As to my generals, there are many more just as brave as Lü Pu, sirs. Whether they live or die, whether they are dismissed or promoted depends entirely on a word from me. It'll be as easy seizing the House of Han as picking a pocket – and what's the difficulty in that? I'm going home now to prepare a crown for myself. I'll bide my time. Even so, I'm afraid that if we leave it too long the situation might change. It would be better to bring the occasion forward a few days.

Exeunt TUNG CHO *and* SOLDIERS.

YANG PIAO: Was there ever a more impudent rogue! His one ambition is to usurp the throne. What shall be our plan, Minister?

WANG YÜN:

The single care I had before is now turned into two,
I see that only trouble results from opening one's
mouth too soon.

YANG PIAO: Minister, how are we to seize this scoundrel and keep the House of Han secure?

WANG YÜN:

Wait, let me set my wits to work on some ingenious
and subtle scheme.

YANG PIAO: Ah, Minister, I see you are no lesser man than the sages of old. We need only do away with Lü Pu. Then it'll be easy to lay hands on Tung Cho.

WANG YÜN:

You may say 'lay hands on Tung Cho',
But how are we to do away with Lü Pu?

YANG PIAO: It all depends upon what scheme you intend to use.

WANG YÜN [*sighs*]: Be patient, Field Marshal. Let me think about it.

YANG PIAO: It must be done within a few days. It is essential that it should be done soon or we will endanger our chance of success.

WANG YÜN:

I know the courses of sun and moon,
But this struggle between dragon and tiger,
Like bow with aim unknown
Draws at my heart. *Exit.*

YANG PIAO: Now he's gone, Wang Yün is bound to hit upon some scheme for us to lay hands on Tung Cho and keep the

House of Han secure in the land. I'll go secretly and report this to His Majesty. *Exit.*

ACT TWO

Enter TUNG CHO *with* LI JU, LI SU *and* SOLDIERS.

TUNG CHO: What impudence is this! Wang Yün told me that he and his fellows would choose a day of good omen soon and come and see me presented to the throne. I see from the Yellow Almanac that there are a great many days of good omen, and still they do not come. Why? Someone go to the gate. When Wang Yün and the others arrive, report to me.

SOLDIER: Yes, Your Excellency.

Enter the Immortal T'AI PO *holding a roll of cloth.*

T'AI PO [*to the audience*]: You people of the mortal world, take your vow and follow me, a poor Taoist priest. Each one of you I shall make immortal, and each one of you I shall bring to understand the Great Way. Let there be no one left here in this world. I am the Immortal T'ai Po. I know the good and evil in men, and can foretell honour and disgrace in the world. I have just returned from an audience with the Emperor of Heaven. I see that in the world below Tung Cho has usurped the power of Emperor Hsien and is plotting to overthrow the House of Han. The Emperor of Heaven is angry and all the gods and goddesses are displeased. They have sent me to see if I can turn him back to the True Way and bring him back to his senses again. This is the gate of Tung Cho's house. [*laughs*] Ha, ha, ha! You are getting too ambitious, Prime Minister Tung Cho. [*weeps*] Oh, oh, oh! You will die very soon, Prime Minister Tung Cho.

Enter a SOLDIER.

SOLDIER: There's a mad priest outside, Your Excellency. He stood there looking at the gate of your residence, and gave out three loud laughs and then three loud sobs. He wouldn't even go away when we beat him.

TUNG CHO: Is that so? Let me go out and see for myself.

TUNG CHO *sees* T'AI PO.

T'AI PO: Oh, oh, oh! You will die very soon, Tung Cho.

TUNG CHO: It's nothing but a mad priest talking nonsense! Arrest him. [*They try to seize him but fail.*] I'll arrest him myself. [T'AI PO *throws the roll of cloth at* TUNG CHO *and goes off.*] Ah, he nearly killed me. What's happened, has he gone? Let me see what it was he hit me with. [TUNG CHO *picks up the roll.*] So it's a roll of cloth. At each end there's the word 'mouth'. And on the cloth there are two lines of verse.

'For a thousand leagues the grass is green.
The oracle prophesies ten long lives.'

Do you understand what it means, Li Ju?

LI JU: I've studied it carefully, Prime Minister, but I can't make head or tail of it. There's no one apart from Ts'ai Yung who'll be able to fathom it out.

TUNG CHO: You're quite right, my son. Call Ts'ai Yung for me, Li Su.

LI SU: Where's Ts'ai Yung?

Enter TS'AI YUNG.

TS'AI YUNG: You sent for me, Prime Minister. What is your wish?

TUNG CHO: A mad priest stood looking at the gate of

my residence and gave out three loud laughs, then three loud sobs. When I went out to see him he threw something straight at my head. Just as I was about to order someone to arrest him he turned into a shaft of golden light and vanished from sight. Here is the thing he threw. I can't understand it. So I've sent for you to have a look at it.

TS'AI YUNG: Very well, if that's the case, please let me see it. Oh, it's a roll of cloth, some ten feet long, with two lines of verse on it.

> 'For a thousand leagues the grass is green.
> The oracle prophesies ten long lives.'

[*aside*] The old scoundrel is going to die at the hand of Lü Pu. It means nothing less than this. [*aloud*] Prime Minister, as I interpret it, above the word 'thousand' there is the word 'grass' and under the word 'thousand' there is the word 'leagues'; doesn't this mean your surname Tung? Under the word 'oracle' there is the word 'prophesy', and under the word 'prophesy' there is the word 'ten'; isn't that your other name – Cho? And as to the roll, at both ends there's the word 'mouth'. If you put one 'mouth' on top of the other 'mouth', doesn't this make the word Lü? And 'cloth' is Pu, is it not? So here we have Lü Pu. The cloth is ten feet long. This means that Your Excellency will attain complete happiness and all will be brought about by the hero Lü Pu. Such is the will of Heaven and the endeavour of men.

TUNG CHO [*smiles*]: What you have said is very much to the point. If I succeed in this great affair, you shall be given the seat of Minister of the Left.

TS'AI YUNG: I am afraid the prime minister might forget.

TUNG CHO: You are right. As the old saying has it, 'The

higher a man is, the more things he forgets.' Keep this roll of cloth. If I am successful, produce it and the position of Minister of the Left will be yours.

TS'AI YUNG: I am very grateful, Prime Minister. I humbly take my leave. I'm outside the gate now. It's for the sake of my parents that I'm obliged to work for Tung Cho. I'll take this roll of cloth and go secretly to Minister Wang's house and consult with him. *Exit.*

TUNG CHO: Has Ts'ai Yung gone? Oh, isn't this almost too good to be true!

> I can trust for everything to my child Lü Pu,
> This great event will be accomplished today.
> Now I believe if a man's intentions are good,
> Heaven will truly help him on his way. *Exeunt.*

Enter WANG YÜN.

WANG YÜN: Tung Cho is extremely powerful, and Lü Pu so brave that a force of ten thousand warriors is helpless before him. I have been turning the matter over and over in my mind but I cannot think of any plan. What's to be done? It's getting dark. I'll close the gate.

Enter TS'AI YUNG.

TS'AI YUNG: This is the minister's house. I'll call someone to open the gate. Open the gate!

WANG YÜN *comes out of the gate.*

WANG YÜN: Who is that calling?

TS'AI YUNG: It's Ts'ai Yung.

WANG YÜN [*sees* TS'AI YUNG]: What brings you here?

TS'AI YUNG: A humble official would not come for nothing.

While Prime Minister Tung Cho was at home in his private residence a begging priest stood looking at his gate, and gave three loud laughs, then three loud sobs. This infuriated the prime minister, but when he ordered him to be arrested the priest threw something at him, then turned into a shaft of golden light and vanished. This is the thing he hit the prime minister with. Have a look at it if you will, Minister.

WANG YÜN: Oh, so it's a roll of cloth with two lines of verse on it. Isn't this the name of Tung Cho?

TS'AI YUNG: You interpret it correctly.

WANG YÜN: The roll of cloth has the word 'mouth' at each end. Evidently this signifies the name of Lü Pu. But the cloth is neither nine feet nor eleven feet long. What does it mean? I don't understand it.

TS'AI YUNG: What's the difficulty? This roll is exactly ten feet long. This means that the days of Tung Cho are numbered. Soon he shall die, and when he dies he will die at the hand of Lü Pu.

WANG YÜN: You must be mistaken. Lü Pu is Tung Cho's foster son. How is he likely to kill Tung Cho?

TS'AI YUNG: Minister, there is only one man before whom you stand and ten thousand before whom you sit. If you could only set Lü Pu against Tung Cho you need consider Tung Cho no more. I am an official of little ability but I am willing to offer you a plan – I call it a Stratagem of Interlocking Rings. It's getting dark now. Permit me to take my leave. *Exit.*

WANG YÜN: What he says is right. But how are we to set about it? A Stratagem of Interlocking Rings! He has left me more puzzled than ever. How maddening! Where is it all to end?

I hate this constant wariness as if the heavens were about to fall,
The constant fear his presence holds as if at a tiger's side one slept.
Truly, like clouds the affairs of men have a thousand transformations,
In a trice a rosy hue will fade and a hoary grey will threaten.
Many times I have prayed to Heaven,
But alas! Heaven is remote from the world of men,
It will not ease our lot.
How sad! that this heart of mine true as iron or stone
Should come to nothing.

I'm tired. I shall go into the garden at the back of the house and take a walk. Here is the Pavilion of Peonies. Bring me the *ch'in.*

Enter a SERVANT BOY *with a* ch'in; *he hands it to* WANG YÜN.

WANG YÜN [*sighs*]: Alas! The House of Han is about to fall. No human power can save it.

WANG YÜN *plays the* ch'in; *enter* TIAO CH'AN, *followed by* MEI-HSIANG.

TIAO CH'AN: I am Tiao Ch'an. During the Revolt of the Yellow Turbans I was separated from my husband Lü Pu, and so it happened that I came to live here. I was fortunate to meet Minister Wang who treats me as though I were his own daughter. It is only this matter of my husband that I find difficult to tell him. The moon is bright and all is quiet. There is no one about. I've taken advantage of this opportunity to come into the garden with Mei-hsiang to offer up some incense to Heaven.

MEI-HSIANG: Come along.

WANG YÜN *sees them and turns aside.*

Shall I set the table near the bed of peonies?

TIAO CH'AN [*breathlessly*]: Mei-hsiang, bring the incense.

MEI-HSIANG: Everything is ready.

TIAO CH'AN:

> Like two lotus flowers on a single stem apart across
> a pool,
> I have borne this separation many years.
> Like two lovebirds who have lost a wing we cannot
> come together.
> With this offering of fragrant incense
> I pray to Heaven.

I am Tiao Ch'an. I am the wife of Lü Pu. We were parted from each other in the city of Lin-t'ao and I have come to live in the house of the minister Wang Yün. But I don't know what has become of Lü Pu. I pray to Heaven that as husband and wife we may soon be united again. [*bows deeply twice*]

MEI-HSIANG: I'll burn some incense for you too. Heaven! I have heard people say that among men there is none to compare with Lü Pu, and among women none to compare with Tiao Ch'an. If you will unite them both soon, it will not be for nothing that they are known as the most perfect match. And it'll benefit me too.

WANG YÜN:

> I had thought she was thin and ailing but from some
> bitter complaint,
> In fact she is sad and restless from the long torment of
> love.

Now I can believe it, the boldness of love knows no bounds!

TIAO CH'AN *weeps.*

What are you doing here, Tiao Ch'an? You are very daring!

MEI-HSIANG: We are discovered. The minister has heard everything.

TIAO CH'AN: I haven't said anything. I only came here because of my health, to burn some incense to Heaven.

WANG YÜN: Silence!

Just now you burnt incense and bowed in appeal to Heaven,
Deeply did reverence and from your own lips spoke your prayer.
Tell me, is a heart so devout and a mind so determined
Merely to ensure that you be healthy and well?

TIAO CH'AN: I had no other purpose. When I saw such fine weather and so pleasant a night my only thought was to worship the moon and offer up incense. I wouldn't dare to say anything else.

WANG YÜN:

Ah!
You spoke of being reunited in love.
Who has separated the twin flying swallows,
Who has broken the lotus flowers' stem,
Who has brought you a lifetime of grief?

TIAO CH'AN: I said none of these things.

WANG YÜN: Do you still deny it?

I only ask you how this misfortune came about,
That you must bear this separation.
In what year?

TIAO CH'AN: Because of my health I came to worship the moon and offer up incense. Truly I had no other purpose.

WANG YÜN:

The wrong in your heart
Became words at your lips,
Every murmur a cry 'Heaven, have you no pity!'

MEI-HSIANG: She said nothing of the sort. If I lie turn me into a pekingese.

WANG YÜN: Hold your tongue!

You said Lü Pu was the most handsome of men,
And Tiao Ch'an the most beautiful of women.

TIAO CH'AN: I said nothing, truly.

WANG YÜN: I heard you say you wished you and your husband might be reunited again soon, Tiao Ch'an. Who is your husband? Tell me the truth. If there's a word of a lie in it I'll have you beaten to death. You'll not get away with it.

TIAO CH'AN [*falls at his feet*]: Don't be angry, my lord. Listen to me. I'm not a native of this city but of the village of Mu-erh in Hsin-chou, a daughter of Rên Ang, and my name is Hung-ch'ang. When Emperor Ling was selecting women for his palace I was one of those chosen, and when I was brought there I was made Mistress of Sable and Cicada Hats, and so I came to be called Tiao Ch'an. Emperor Ling bestowed me upon Ting Chien-yang, who gave me in marriage to Lü Pu. Afterwards, during the Revolt of the Yellow Turbans, Lü Pu and I were separated from each other. I didn't know what had become of him. I had the good fortune to be taken into your house and to be treated as your own daughter – a favour I can never hope to repay. Yesterday when mother and I were in the room upstairs overlooking the streets we saw soldiers marching by, and on his famous charger the Red Hare there sat Lü Pu himself. So I came to offer up incense and pray that as husband and wife we may be reunited again soon. I never expected that you would hear me. I deserve to be severely punished.

WANG YÜN: Is this the truth, Tiao Ch'an?

TIAO CH'AN: I dare not tell a lie, my lord.

WANG YÜN: Ah ha! Ts'ai Yung, how ingenious of you! Isn't this the Stratagem of Interlocking Rings? It all turns on this woman.

> Thus Heaven's will shapes itself to men's designs.
> There is no need to look for another plan,
> No need to confront him face to face,
> No need to engage him in a fight.
> This miraculous stratagem can encompass all.
> Now the people will be released from their plight,
> From now on the rule of the House of Han will be secure.
> If a word of this stratagem were to be winded abroad
> It would mean the end of my family one and all.
> I am worried, I am worried – mind confused, heart astir.
> Who would dream that this woman was to be found in our house?
> One day soon a feast shall be held,
> And war shall lie hidden in a field of fair looks.
> Who could escape such a stratagem as this?

Tiao Ch'an, if you will obey me in one thing I will reunite you with your husband.

TIAO CH'AN: One thing, my lord! If it were ten your child would obey. But what is this one thing?

WANG YÜN: I remember that at the time of the Warring States several hundred years ago, there was a certain Chuan Chu, a man of great courage, who only accomplished his great deeds through the help of his wife. During the present reign there was the mother of Wang Ling who took her own life by swallowing a dagger, commanding her son to serve the House of Han and no other. Afterwards the names of both of them were recorded in history. Everyone sang their praises and spoke of their deeds. Now if you are willing to carry out a scheme of mine that will deliver Tung Cho into my hands and restore the House of Han to power, then I will ensure that you and your husband are reunited for ever. You must not mind if the fat Tung Cho makes advances to you, my child. You will gain an illustrious name for ten thousand generations to come for having saved an emperor.

TIAO CH'AN: I will do whatever you wish, father.

WANG YÜN: Very well. Go back to the inner hall for the present.

TIAO CH'AN: Yes, father.

> If I would have history bear some trace of mine,
> Should I mourn to have my beauty serve another.

Exeunt TIAO CH'AN *and* MEI-HSIANG.

WANG YÜN: Where's Chi Lü? [*Enter* CHI LÜ.] Chi Lü, go first and tell the steward to prepare a feast, then go to the house of Count Lü Pu next to the prime minister's and invite him to come. [*Exit* CHI LÜ.] I've no doubt Lü Pu will come to my feast; and when he comes I shall know what to do.

If I don't cast in a pool ten thousand feet deep,
How else is this great turtle to bite? *Exit.*

Enter LÜ PU *with* SOLDIERS.

LÜ PU: I am Lü Pu. At the Tiger Cage Pass I once defeated eighteen armies of the feudal princes. My prowess shook the whole kingdom and they made me a count. Apart from fighting battles I do nothing but drink and have a good time. There's nothing to do in the barracks today. I wonder if someone will come and invite me out.

Enter CHI LÜ.

CHI LÜ: Will someone report that a messenger from Minister Wang asks to see the count.

A SOLDIER *reports.*

LÜ PU: Send him in. [CHI LÜ *sees* LÜ PU.] What brings you here, Chi Lü?

CHI LÜ: The minister ordered me to come. He says that since there's been little news from the frontier recently he has had a small feast prepared, if Your Grace will condescend to join him.

LÜ PU [*smiles*]: I say! the old fellow knows he can't give me the cold shoulder for long. You go ahead. I'll follow right away.

CHI LÜ: I'll go and tell my master. It's hoped Your Grace will come early. *Exit.*

LÜ PU: Come, saddle my horse someone. *Exeunt.*

Enter WANG YÜN *with* CHI LÜ *and* ATTENDANTS.

WANG YÜN: Send someone to the gate. When Lü Pu comes let me know immediately.

Enter LÜ PU *with* SOLDIERS.

LÜ PU: This is the gate of Minister Wang's house. Someone take care of my horse.

CHI LÜ *reports;* WANG YÜN *hurries out in welcome.*

WANG YÜN: If I had known that Your Grace would arrive so early I would have come further to welcome you.

LÜ PU: You're an old minister of the court, Wang Yün. Why do you stand on such ceremony with me? You are too humble. I'm afraid I'm not worthy of it.

WANG YÜN: I dare not do otherwise. I am greatly honoured that Your Grace should accept my invitation. Bring in the feast.

CHI LÜ *brings in the banqueting table;*
WANG YÜN *offers a cup of wine to* LÜ PU.

Please Your Grace, take this cup of wine.

LÜ PU: What virtue, what talent do I have, Minister, that you should have wine and a feast prepared to entertain me in this fashion? How is it I deserve all this?

WANG YÜN:

I fear I'm but a petty official of no particular talent.
How should such as I receive a prince at my table?

LÜ PU: Minister, you have invited me to this feast. What's the reason behind it?

WANG YÜN: No reason other than to honour your illustrious name.

May Your Grace have an escort of a thousand soldiers,
May Your Grace be given the lordship of eight cities,
May Your Grace hold the seal of commander-in-chief,
May Your Grace have an early summons from the Emperor.

LÜ PU [*laughs*]: I'm grateful for your good wishes, Minister. I'm only afraid I won't have the good fortune to enjoy them.

WANG YÜN: I've studied astrology since I was a child, and I can tell the days of the House of Han are numbered. The great virtues and achievements of the prime minister are there for everyone to see. The day is near at hand when he is sure to mount the throne. I only hope Your Grace will help to have me promoted.

LÜ PU: Rest assured, Minister. If the prime minister succeeds no one could fill the position of Minister of the Left better than you.

WANG YÜN: Thank you, Your Grace, thank you. Please, drink this cup of wine.

LÜ PU: I am drinking too fast. Wait, let me drink a cup or two slowly.

WANG YÜN: It's often been well said that if there's no music at a feast the pleasure is not complete. Someone send word to the inner hall and ask the young mistress Tiao Ch'an to come here.

Enter TIAO CH'AN *followed by* MEI-HSIANG.

TIAO CH'AN: What is it, father?

WANG YÜN: Child, Lü Pu is in the front hall, slightly drunk. Pretend not to recognize him. Hand him a cup of wine and sing him a song. Then see what he says.

TIAO CH'AN: Yes, father.

WANG YÜN [*leads* TIAO CH'AN *to* LÜ PU]: Young mistress, pay your respects to the count.

TIAN CH'AN [*bows*[1]]: Ten thousand greetings, Your Grace.

LÜ PU [*at once returning her courtesy*]: Young mistress, no ceremony I beg you!

WANG YÜN: A cup of wine for His Grace, child.

TIAO CH'AN: Bring the wine.

MEI-HSIANG: Here you are.

TIAO CH'AN *offers wine to* LÜ PU.

TIAO CH'AN: Drink this cup of wine, Your Grace.

LÜ PU *takes the wine and drinks.*

LÜ PU: Minister, I am drunk. I'm sorry, this is against all the rules. I've had enough wine.

WANG YÜN: Drink up to your heart's content. If you get drunk what does it matter! Sing a song, child, while the count drinks.

TIAO CH'AN [*sings*]:

When I was young I served the Emperor
Who gave me to be a hero's wife.
But midstream a storm arose
And divided us three years,
Each anxious and each far apart.
Then we only thought to flee the war's commotion;
Now years of peace have brought prosperity,
I hoped we should be joined in love again and in giving thanks to Heaven.
But now that we meet face to face,
Can it be that you have forgotten Tiao Ch'an?

LÜ PU [*recognizes* TIAO CH'AN]: Isn't this Tiao Ch'an? How does she come to be here?

WANG YÜN [*aside*]: It's true then. The fellow has fallen into the trap.

> She, eyes speak her love and blushes veil her lovely face.
> He, he cannot sit still or give his mind to the fine feast,
> Loosening his clothing,
> Turning this way and that.

LÜ PU: Minister, please forgive me for losing control of myself like this.

WANG YÜN: Feel free to do as you wish, Your Grace.

LÜ PU *is sick.*

LÜ PU: I'm drunk and I've made a mess of your magnificent hall. This is unforgivable.

WANG YÜN:

> You've done no such thing.

Please, be seated. I've one or two matters to attend to.

WANG YÜN *withdraws.*

LÜ PU [*softly*]: The minister has gone. Tiao Ch'an?

TIAO CH'AN: Yes.

LÜ PU: How do you come to be here, wife?

TIAO CH'AN: After we were parted from each other in Ling-t'ao I came to live here in the minister's house. Who would ever have thought that today we should see each other again. I have almost broken my heart for you. [*weeps*]

LÜ PU [*hiding his tears*]: And I almost died of longing for you, Tiao Ch'an.

WANG YÜN *hurries forward.*

WANG YÜN: What's that you two were saying?

LÜ PU *and* TIAO CH'AN *fall at his feet.*

LÜ PU: I'm very drunk.

TIAO CH'AN: I didn't say anything.

WANG YÜN: Hold your tongue, girl!

LÜ PU: It's all my fault. It has nothing to do with Tiao Ch'an.

WANG YÜN:

> You look on me as if I were the plague!
> In all good will I lay a feast before you,
> And you come here pandering your looks for love.

LÜ PU: Minister, I'm afraid you don't understand. Let me explain to you. Tiao Ch'an was married to me. We were separated from each other during the Revolt of the Yellow Turbans and ever since I haven't known where she was. In fact she was here in your house, Minister. Having been separated from her so long I was overwhelmed with emotion. I hope you will take pity, Minister, and reunite us as husband and wife. I will not forget your goodness as long as I live and I will do anything to repay you.

WANG YÜN: Have you anything to say, my child?

TIAO CH'AN: It is all true. I only hope you will forgive us.

WANG YÜN: Since this is the case, please get up, Your Grace. And you, child, go back to the inner hall. [*Exeunt* TIAO CH'AN *and* MEI-HSIANG.] As you hadn't told me how was I to know? Even if I'd tried I could never have arranged such a marriage. I shall choose a day of good omen and give Tiao Ch'an to you with a dowry of three million pieces of silver. What do you say to that?

LÜ PU: I am most grateful to you, Minister. Tiao Ch'an's father shall be my father.

WANG YÜN: There is one thing, Your Grace. I am afraid that when the prime minister comes to hear of this, won't he think I acted improperly?

LÜ PU: That doesn't matter. He'll be all the more glad when he knows.

WANG YÜN: Well, within the next few days I'll arrange another feast and invite the prime minister, first to discuss some important business of ours and then to mention the matter of your marriage. Won't that be the best way to proceed?

LÜ PU: Father-in-law, this is more than one could ask. I shall never dare forget it as long as I live. Enough of wine! Permit me to take my leave.

WANG YÜN: I hope nothing's been neglected, Your Grace.

LÜ PU: Not at all, not at all. *Exit.*

WANG YÜN: Chi Lü, go to the prime minister's residence and say that Wang Yün invites the prime minister to a feast. If he declines you may say that I have invited him especially to discuss some important business, and hope that nothing will prevent him from coming.

CHI LÜ: I understand.

WANG YÜN: I daresay Tung Cho is only a simple soldier. When he hears it's to discuss some important business he is sure to come.

> I must use my wits and show my skill,
> An eye to advantage is the essence of power.
> Songs shall be sung and pipes and strings play,
> With flowers like brocade and a river of wine,
> Myself all the more humble, my mien gentle and kind,
> So shall Tung Cho be made half crazy with wine;
> He is sure to fall in love with the first morsel he sees.

At that moment I shall beguile him with the lovely
Tiao Ch'an.
Secretly I make this vow to Heaven.

You ask me what this vow is?

To do away with this scoundrel as soon as I can,
And prove myself to the world a loyal and honourable
man.
Exeunt.

ACT THREE

Enter TUNG CHO *and* ATTENDANTS.

TUNG CHO: Only a few days and they'll invite me to mount the throne! All this time it's been, why haven't I heard from them yet? The old scoundrel Yang Piao is a very headstrong fellow. Well, let him be! But Wang Yün, is he trying to make a fool of me too?

Enter CHI LÜ.

CHI LÜ: Here I am at the gate. Will someone announce that Chi Lü is at the gate with a message from Minister Wang?

An ATTENDANT *reports.*

TUNG CHO: Tell him to come in.
ATTENDANT: Come this way.

CHI LÜ *sees* TUNG CHO.

TUNG CHO: What brings you here, Chi Lü?
CHI LÜ: My master Wang Yün has requested me to come and invite Your Excellency to a feast.
TUNG CHO: I've something very important to discuss with my colleagues, Chi Lü. A feast at Wang Yün's! Go back

and tell the old fellow Wang Yün I've no time for his feast!

CHI LÜ: Prime Minister, my master said that his only reason for holding this feast was to invite Your Excellency to discuss an important matter of business.

TUNG CHO: Oh, so he is inviting me to discuss an important matter of business. You go ahead, Chi Lü. I'll follow at once. [*Exit* CHI LÜ.] Get my carriage ready. [*smiles*] If events take an unpleasant turn in the course of the feast I'll finish the old fellow off on the spot. *Exeunt.*

Enter WANG YÜN *with* ATTENDANTS.

WANG YÜN: The old villain Tung Cho will soon be here.

Today the decorated hall has a different air.
Abode of brocade and embroidered robes,
It hides a secret field of war,
Except there are no tigerish warriors,
Only a lovely woman led to a lavish feast.
With hidden bow and poisoned arrow I need only wait
my prey,
And spread my net to catch the game.
This shall be no ordinary feast.

Enter TUNG CHO *followed by* LI JU, LI SU *and* SOLDIERS.

TUNG CHO:

I've no need to suspect this feast at Wang Yun's,
Any intrigue and I'm immediately told.
Let me hear so much as a word out of line
And I'll reduce his whole house to a cesspool.

You soldiers stay at the gate.

Enter CHI LÜ.

CHI LÜ [*nervously*]: The prime minister has arrived, master.

WANG YÜN: I'll go myself to welcome him.

WANG YÜN *sees* TUNG CHO *and falls at his feet.*

I am greatly honoured by your presence in my humble home. I haven't come far enough to welcome you – I beg you, spare my life.

TUNG CHO: Minister Wang, you hold a very high position in the government. To see you kneeling down in the street passers-by will think it in very bad taste. Please get up.

WANG YÜN: This is no more than is due, Your Excellency. I have invited you to this feast today, Prime Minister, because if I were to delay it several days more you would have mounted the throne, and then our positions – yours as emperor, mine as subject – would be as far-removed from each other as heaven from earth; there would never be another chance of enjoying such fellowship. It is for this reason I make so bold as to invite you. I hope Your Excellency will not think it amiss.

TUNG CHO [*bursts out laughing*]: I'm only afraid I'll not reach that position.

WANG YÜN: Bring in the feast. [CHI LÜ *brings in the banqueting table;* WANG YÜN *offers* TUNG CHO *a cup of wine.*] Drink this cup of wine, Your Excellency.

TUNG CHO: Wait a minute. I'm ready to drink and I'm ready to talk! But first tell me, this business of the Gate of the Silver Terrace, when is it to be exactly? Tell me the date and I'll drink.

WANG YÜN: I can report to Your Excellency that the matter has been decided. It will be within the next three days.

TUNG CHO: If it's only a matter of three days there's no cause to worry, is there? Bring the wine, Minister. Now I can drink, indeed I can drink!

WANG YÜN [*offering wine*]: Come, Prime Minister, drink the three cups of wine, then let us begin the feast.

TUNG CHO [*after drinking three cups of wine*]: All these high officials in the court, let them displease me a little and I'll put out their eyes; displease me a lot and I'll cut off their heads; worse than that and I'll wipe out their clan. But you, old fellow, you know how to conduct yourself, your manner is humble, your speech unassuming. That's very much to my liking.

WANG YÜN: Thank you for speaking so highly of me, Prime Minister.

TUNG CHO: If I am successful I shall see that you are placed in the highest rank and promoted above all the feudal princes. And what official position should be given to Li Su?

WANG YÜN:

Let Li Su be made General of the Vanguard.

TUNG CHO: Yes. And my child Lü Pu? What official position for him?

WANG YÜN:

Lü Pu should have the gold tent of commander-in-chief.

TUNG CHO: That will be very fitting. [*smiles*] And you, Minister, what position would you like?

WANG YÜN:

I have only known books and court affairs.
I have never worn armour or fought in the field of war.

TUNG CHO: Even so, what would you like to be truly?

WANG YÜN:

> I hope Your Excellency might make me a counsellor of the first rank.

TUNG CHO: Is this the reason you've invited me? Because of this official position? Don't worry. If this great affair is concluded within the next few days the position of Minister of the Left will certainly be yours.

WANG YÜN [*bows low in thanks*]: I hope Your Excellency will not forget what you have said today. Someone bring some more wine.

CHI LÜ: Here you are.

WANG YÜN [*offering a cup of wine with both hands*]: Please, Prime Minister, take another cup of wine.

TUNG CHO: Just a moment. This wine is strong, and the weather is hot. I feel a little drowsy. I'll rest for a while.

TUNG CHO *drops off to sleep.*

WANG YÜN: The prime minister is drunk. Go and tell them in the inner hall and ask Mei-hsiang to accompany Tiao Ch'an out to fan the prime minister. [*Enter* TIAO CH'AN, *holding a fan, followed by* MEI-HSIANG.] Tung Cho has drunk too much, my child, and fallen asleep in the front hall. Go and fan him, will you.

> Her hair shines brightly dressed with oil,
> Her powdered face smells sweet,
> Her eyebrows new styled like crescent moons,
> Her fairy gown newspun of silk of the tenderest lotus threads.

TUNG CHO [*awakes*]: Ah, what a cool breeze! Who is that fanning me? [*sees* TIAO CH'AN] What a woman! How often does the world see beauty like this! Is she some immortal from Heaven? What a woman, what a woman! Come nearer. Let you and me drink a few cups of wine together.

TIAO CH'AN *makes a gesture of embarrassment.*

WANG YÜN [*aside*]: The evil old scoundrel couldn't help but fall into the trap.

I see the cups rattling as the villain offers her wine.

TUNG CHO: What a beautiful woman! I've thousands of women at home but none of them can compare with her. How does this old fellow come to have such a gem in his keeping?

WANG YÜN:

He casts his eyes intently over her shimmering form.

TUNG CHO [*pulls* TIAO CH'AN *to him*]: Come nearer! I won't harm you.

WANG YÜN:

I see Tiao Ch'an blushing, hating to be drawn to his side.

TUNG CHO: What a beautiful woman!

WANG YÜN:

The old villain's mouth waters for staring at her so hard.

TUNG CHO: What a beautiful woman! Come a little nearer!

WANG YÜN:

Already the villain has fallen into the trap.

TUNG CHO: This woman was born with a face lovely enough to make fish drown themselves and wild geese fall from the sky. Her beauty is enough to make the moon hide her face and flowers hang their heads. Oh, what a beautiful woman! Ah, what a cool breeze! Young woman, come nearer, fan harder! [TIAO CH'AN *throws down the fan and goes off;* TUNG CHO *runs after her.*] Wang Yün, what woman was that fanning me a moment ago?

WANG YÜN: My daughter, and she is not engaged to anyone yet.

TUNG CHO: So she's your daughter, is she? Then why did you ask her to fan me?

WANG YÜN: People in ancient times often showed respect for their guests by sending their wives or sons to wait upon them, and didn't think it improper. Moreover I've pledged my life to you. Why should I begrudge you a woman?

TUNG CHO: If I succeed in this great affair within the coming few days the only thing I shall be wanting, Minister, is a good wife like her. If you're willing to give her to me, won't this make the event doubly perfect?

WANG YÜN: If you don't object to my daughter's unworthy appearance, I am happy to give her to you to be one of your concubines.

TUNG CHO: How can you say concubine? She shall be my wife. Even then I'm only afraid I'm not worthy of her. [*takes off his jade belt*] Since you've done me the honour of giving your consent, may I offer this jade belt as a token of the engagement?

WANG YÜN [*taking it*]: Thank you, Your Excellency.

TUNG CHO: Today is a special day, Minister. Since you've given your daughter to be my wife, you'll soon be the imperial father-in-law and I your son-in-law. A son-in-law is a son, so you will be my father. Father, please sit down and accept your son's respects. [*bows low to him;* WANG

YÜN *returns the courtesy*] There is one thing more, though I hardly dare say it.

WANG YÜN: What is your command, Prime Minister?

TUNG CHO: Since you've promised to give me your daughter in marriage she is a member of my family now. Ask her to come out again and pour me another cup of wine. That's in order, isn't it?

WANG YÜN: When the prime minister commands who dares to disobey? Chi Lü, send word to the inner hall and ask Tiao Ch'an to come at once. [*Enter* TIAO CH'AN.] Show your respects to the prime minister, child. Offer him a cup of wine.

TIAO CH'AN *offers wine to* TUNG CHO.

TUNG CHO [*laughs*]: My wife offers me wine! Wine! If it were urine I would drink it! Bring a large cup. If you don't have a large cup bring a footbath! What a beautiful woman! What a beautiful woman! The more I look at her the more beautiful I find her. I've had enough wine, I can't drink any more. I am sure tomorrow is an auspicious day. Bring your daughter over and let us be married! I shall be waiting at my residence, father-in-law, especially for you to bring me my wife. And I shall have a small feast prepared also, especially for you. You mustn't let such an auspicious day pass and keep me in anticipation any longer.

WANG YÜN: Since you're sure that tomorrow is an auspicious day I shall prepare a dowry of three million pieces of silver and accompany my daughter to your residence.

TUNG CHO: Tomorrow at the prime minister's residence I shall be waiting. Now permit me to take my leave.

Exeunt TUNG CHO *and his retinue.*

WANG YÜN: Get the carriage ready, Chi Lü, for the young mistress Tiao Ch'an to be sent to the prime minister's residence tomorrow evening. *Exeunt.*

Enter TUNG CHO *with* LI JU, LI SU, ATTENDANTS *and* SERVING MAIDS.

TUNG CHO: Yesterday, Li Ju and Li Su, I ordered you to prepare a feast. Is it ready?

LI JU: It has been ready for a long time.

TUNG CHO: Minister Wang is sending the young mistress Tiao Ch'an here today to be my wife. I was so excited I didn't sleep a wink last night. I have everything ready for the marriage ceremony, there's nothing that hasn't been done. It is getting dark. They will soon be here.

Enter WANG YÜN *with* TIAO CH'AN *in a carriage; drums, music.*

WANG YÜN: Someone report to the prime minister that Wang Yün is at the gate.

LI SU: Wang Yün has brought his daughter to be married to you.

TUNG CHO: Quick, ask them please to come in. [*sees* WANG YÜN *and smiles*] You have kept your word, father-in-law. You're a good man, I say. Now where's my wife?

WANG YÜN: In the carriage.

TUNG CHO: Please, come down from the carriage. You women, look after her well. Go with her to the inner hall and dress her for the ceremony. [*Exit* TIAO CH'AN *with* SERVING MAIDS.] Bring wine. Drink this cup of wine, father-in-law, I beg you.

WANG YÜN: I dare not, Prime Minister. You drink first, please.

TUNG CHO: I beg you, father-in-law, drink.

WANG YÜN [*drinks*]: Now Prime Minister, please, you take a cup.

TUNG CHO: Come. I'll drink a cup. Hand me another. I don't care if I drink until dawn. Only tonight I have something else to do. Allow me to entertain you another day. I hope you'll excuse me.

WANG YÜN: Then permit me to take my leave. *Exit.*

TUNG CHO: Li Ju, serve the feast in the inner hall. My wife and I shall exchange a marriage cup. *Exeunt.*

Enter LÜ PU.

LÜ PU: Minister Wang said that tonight he would bring Tiao Ch'an here and make her my wife. I didn't expect to see this, a carriage and musicians, and servants carrying boxes, all going into the prime minister's residence, and no sign of Minister Wang coming out. I wonder, is the old villain plotting some treachery? I'll wait here at the gate until Wang Yün comes out. Then I'll see what he has to say.

Enter WANG YÜN.

WANG YÜN: Now the old scoundrel's gone into the inner hall.

LÜ PU: I've been waiting here a long time, Minister.

WANG YÜN: Quiet!

Thinking only to be with the night moon at the
  Western Chamber,
Both father and son aspire to be grooms,
And engage in this absurd and unseemly display.

LÜ PU: Minister, your daughter is in fact my wife, who happens to have taken lodging in your house. Yesterday at the feast you yourself promised me that she should be mine. Today you send her to the prime minister's residence. What is the reason for this?

WANG YÜN:

> You wag your tongue and flap your lips, declaring
> this and that –
> The bride is in her carriage,
> She cannot see her former love with two-pronged
> spear and blazoned saddle,
> But curses and reproaches me.
> In vain your shows of strength, your feats of arms,
> Your pursuit of loyalty and fine ideals
> For uniting the kingdom and bringing peace to the
> realm.
> You would allow Tung Cho like a mewing owl
> To spread his wings like a bird of prey
> And take Tiao Ch'an to wife by force.

LÜ PU: But Minister, where exactly is your daughter now?

WANG YÜN: Your Grace is ignorant of the facts. I invited the prime minister to feast with me yesterday, and mentioned this impending marriage of yours. The prime minister could not have been more pleased and said, 'Call the young woman here and let me have a look at her.' So there was nothing I could do but call Tiao Ch'an. Four times she bowed to him. Suddenly at the sight of her beauty up rose the beast in the villain. Today when the carriage came to the gate of the residence he sent a group of serving maids who took Tiao Ch'an from the carriage and hustled her into the inner hall. Count, you are no man if you don't take action on your wife's behalf. What use are you otherwise? Who's ever heard of a father-in-law making a daughter-in-law his concubine by force? Pah! It's too shameful for words!

LÜ PU: If you hadn't told me, Minister, how was I to know? How could the villain do such an odious thing? It's enough to make one's blood boil!

WANG YÜN:

> Lü Pu, I see you are indeed a valiant general.
> Who can withstand your spear,
> You whose fame spreads beyond the Tiger Cage Pass,
> In fear of whom the feudal princes stand as if struck dead?
> You are indeed a mighty pillar of the kingdom,
> A beam that spans the seas securing heaven and earth.
> Right and honour are on your side, he has no excuse;
> How should he turn the cloud-capped residence of prime minister
> Into a resort for illicit love-making!

LÜ PU: Tung Cho, you villain, you shameless villain! Tiao Ch'an and I are husband and wife by all the laws of Heaven. That old wretch adopted me as his foster-son. How can there be a law of kinship allowing this?

WANG YÜN: Everybody knows there is no such law.

LÜ PU: Minister, go home now, if you will. If I see Tiao Ch'an tonight I shall find out the truth. I'll not let that villain get away with this! [*Exit* WANG YÜN.] What a bare-faced rogue the fellow is! Taking my Tiao Ch'an by force! I shall go straight to the inner hall and search out the old villain. [*withdraws*]

Enter TUNG CHO *followed by* TIAO CH'AN *and* SERVING MAIDS.

TUNG CHO: What a happy man I am! Bring in the feast. Let my wife hand me a cup of wine, and I'll drink till I'm dead drunk. This should give us some spirit for love! [TIAO CH'AN *hands him wine and* TUNG CHO *drinks.*] Another cup! Give me another cup! Wife, you drink a cup too! Prepare our bed, attendants. My wife and I are about to retire. [*falls asleep*]

LÜ PU *comes forward.*

LÜ PU: This is the front of the old villain's bedchamber. How am I to get Tiao Ch'an out? If only I could see her, then all would be well.

TIAO CH'AN: The old villain is drunk. I've heard people say there's a little side gate in this garden which leads to Lü Pu's quarters. I'll try and find it. Ah, there's a little gate here. I'll push it open.

LÜ PU: Isn't that Tiao Ch'an coming? Wait, let me call her. Tiao Ch'an!

TIAO CH'AN [*sees* LÜ PU]: Isn't that Lü Pu?

LÜ PU: Isn't that Tiao Ch'an?

TIAO CH'AN: Lü Pu, I have almost died of shame! When my carriage came to the gate of your residence the prime minister ordered his servants to take me into his house. Was there ever such a thing as a father-in-law marrying his daughter-in-law? Lü Pu, you are a man, where is your strength and your pride? Why aren't you gnashing your teeth and tearing your hair? Do something for your wife, or what use are you? Pah! are you not ashamed of yourself?

LÜ PU: Wife, everything is clear now. Round from this gate is my house. We'll go and talk there.

TUNG CHO [*awakes*]: Wife, wife! How is it my wife's nowhere to be seen? Where has she gone? [*looks about*] Ah, the side gate, how does that come to be open? My son Lü Pu's house is the other side. I'll look for her there. Wife, where are you?

TIAO CH'AN: Lü Pu, isn't that the old villain coming?

LÜ PU: Don't worry. I'll hide in the shadow of this wall and see what he says. Then the old villain shall have a taste of my fist.

TUNG CHO [*sees* TIAO CH'AN]: Wife, how do you come to be here at Lü Pu's house? Has the brute dared to make advances to you? [*sees* LÜ PU] So he is here, the brute! If I don't make an end of you, Lü Pu, I swear my name is not Tung Cho!

LÜ PU [*strikes* TUNG CHO *a blow*]: I've struck the old villain down. That's no good. I'd better be off! *Exit.*

TUNG CHO *falls to the ground;* TIAO CH'AN *helps him up.*

TUNG CHO: Ah, ah! the brute nearly beat me to death. Where is Li Su?

Enter LI SU.

LI SU: You called, Your Excellency. What would you have of me?

TUNG CHO: That brute Lü Pu, the impudence of him! He's been openly making advances to my wife. When I came upon them, he turned and gave me such a blow that I fell to the ground, and then he ran off. Go and arrest the brute, but be sure to take care. Go as quick as you can, and hurry straight back.

LI SU: I have your orders. I'll have him arrested at once. *Exit.*

TUNG CHO: Wife, my whole body hurts from that fall. Help me back gently to the inner hall.

TIAO CH'AN: It was fortunate that Your Excellency came at that moment, or that fellow was sure to have violated me. Come, Your Excellency, you must take care of yourself.

Exeunt, TIAO CH'AN *helping* TUNG CHO

ACT FOUR

Enter LI SU *in full armour.*

LI SU:

Sharpening my sword I have worn down Mount Tai,
The waters of the North Sea my horse has drunk dry.
A man of thirty with no achievements to claim
Can be called a man in nothing but name.

The prime minister ordered me to capture Lü Pu. I've been following the tracks of his horse along the road and chased him up here. *Exit.*

Enter WANG YÜN.

WANG YÜN: I have set this Stratagem of Interlocking Rings in motion, but I don't know yet how it is working out.

I may have exercised my wits in vain
For those few whose hope was still the House of Han.
As if in endless spite the brass water-clock drips.
The bright moon rises late to the window.
The whole night long I have paced up and down,
Sleep never comes to my eyes.

It's almost midnight. Why isn't there any news?

For Prime Minister Tung the swallows' meet, the orioles' tryst,

A thousandweight of flesh the new bridegroom, and
happy beyond measure.
Count Lü Pu, the lonely phoenix, the solitary *lüan*,
Beyond measure vexed, in love divided from his
former lovely wife.
The pearls of Lady Tiao Ch'an's tears fill full the
phoenix cup,
The storm of Lü Pu's fury tears apart the clustering
doves.
It is for this I am filled with fear and doubt,
Afraid lest by a single leaf the news of spring leak out.

Enter LÜ PU.

LÜ PU: That old villain is bound to send someone to arrest me. I'll lie low for the present in Minister Wang's house and consult with him. I must kill that old scoundrel and snatch Tiao Ch'an back from him. I'll not be satisfied with anything less. This is the gate of Minister Wang's house. Open the gate, open the gate!

WANG YÜN: That sounds like the voice of Lü Pu at the gate. The fellow has fallen into the trap. I'll open the gate and see who it is.

LÜ PU: Minister, it's your child Lü Pu here.

WANG YÜN: Lü Pu. Come into the house and talk. What brings you here at this time of night?

LÜ PU: Minister, because of that old villain's shameless behaviour, I struck him a blow that sent him sprawling to the ground. I've come especially to tell you, Minister. What use is there for people like this treacherous official, this double-dyed villain? It would be far better to think out a plan for me to take my revenge on him.

WANG YÜN:

With all my heart
How can I not be angry for you?
For nothing you have helped him,
Lent him your support.
The world cannot tolerate this Old No-Conscience
Behaving with no more understanding than a mule or horse.
You have done your best for him,
And for your endeavours this is your reward.

LÜ PU: Now I have begun I shall not stop at this. I'll kill the old villain with my own hands.

WANG YÜN: Lü Pu, wait, don't be too rash! Let's take our time and discuss the matter carefully.

Enter LI SU.

LI SU: I've been trailing Lü Pu all the way and followed him here. This is Minister Wang's residence! He must be hiding there. I'll call someone to the gate. Minister, open the gate, open the gate!

LÜ PU: Minister, isn't that Li Su calling at the gate? The old villain must have ordered him to come and arrest me. What am I to do?

WANG YÜN: It's all right. Hide behind the curtain for now. I'll go and open the gate. [*comes forward*]

LI SU: What is the meaning of this, Minister? If you've given your daughter to the prime minister, then let the prime minister have her. If you've given her to Lü Pu, then let her be Lü Pu's. Why this confusion? It's caused a whole night of quarrelling and commotion between father and son. Lü

Pu struck the prime minister a blow that sent him sprawling to the ground, and for a long time he couldn't get up. Now I've brought a party of soldiers on the prime minister's orders, to have Lü Pu arrested. We've followed him all the way and saw him enter your residence. Hand him over at once and don't try to protect him. It won't be only the prime minister who'll be angry; you'll not get away with it with me either, old fellow.

WANG YÜN: Don't be angry, General. I remember your ancestor Li T'ung who killed the usurper Wang Mang and helped to establish the rule of the twelve emperors of the later Han dynasty. For more than two hundred years the House of Han has ruled the kingdom and principally due to your ancestor General Li T'ung. You are a descendant of a loyal servant of the crown, how can you serve under such a treacherous minister? You'll bear the reproach of countless generations for this. Won't it even cast a smear on the reputation of your ancestor Li T'ung? Tiao Ch'an is in fact the wife of Lü Pu. When Tung Cho saw she was possessed of some beauty he forced her to be his concubine. General, if your wife had been taken from you by force, what would your feelings be?

LI SU: Minister, if you hadn't told me, how would I have known? So this is the shameless blackguard he is! It says well for Lü Pu that he can still bear it at all. If it had been me I would have killed the old villain long ago. Where is Lü Pu now? I'll offer him my help and we'll go together and finish off the old villain.

WANG YÜN: Why are you waiting, Your Grace? Come out, won't you?

LÜ PU [*comes out from behind the curtain and kowtows to* LI SU]: I've been almost out of my mind with rage!

LI SU [*helps him up*]: The impudence of the old villain! Let me offer you my help and we'll go and finish off the old villain.

WANG YÜN: Since you are of our mind, General, follow me and let us report to the Emperor. *Exeunt.*

Enter YANG PIAO *with* SOLDIERS.

YANG PIAO: Day and night I've been at my wits' end. I haven't been able to think of any plan. For the last few days I haven't even seen Minister Wang. It's most vexing!

Enter WANG YÜN, LÜ PU *and* LI SU.

WANG YÜN: This is the gate of Yang Piao's house. Someone announce that Wang Yün wishes to see the master.

A SOLDIER *reports to* YANG PIAO; WANG YÜN *comes forward.*

YANG PIAO: Minister, what brings you here in this agitated state?

WANG YÜN: I have Lü Pu and Li Su with me here. They are both ready to do all they can to lay hands on Tung Cho. I came especially to consult with you. The two generals are at the gate.

YANG PIAO: In that case why not ask them to come in? [LÜ PU *and* LI SU *come forward and see* YANG PIAO.] It's a rare thing for two generals to show such loyalty and honour! If you are willing to help the House of Han to seize Tung Cho I shall report this to the Emperor immediately. Naturally you'll be promoted and abundantly rewarded.

LI SU: But sir, there is no one more powerful than Tung Cho. Of all the court, who is there who is not in his clutches? Whatever action we take must be completely secure or we'll be courting disaster. You sir, and you Minister Wang, must quickly decide on a plan, and a plan so swift that like a flash of thunder there'll be no time to stop one's ears. Only that way can we expect success. We two have no more than courage to offer, but if at any point you want to try our mettle, we'll not fail you even if it's a matter of life or death.

YANG PIAO: What you've said is perfectly right. Minister Wang and I have already made a secret plan. You two generals go and lie in ambush near the Gate of the Silver Terrace. Wait there until the Royal Decree has been read out, then you two generals come forward and lay hands on the traitor. That way the great deed will be accomplished and you will have made yourselves a name for all time. [*Exeunt* LÜ PU *and* LI SU.] It's lucky that there's this quarrel between Lü Pu and Tung Cho. It must mean Heaven's hand is in his downfall. Now this business of the enthronement at the Gate of the Silver Terrace, we need someone to fetch him and accompany him to the palace. Which of the officials would it be best to ask?

WANG YÜN: It must be Ts'ai Yung. Then the old scoundrel will have no suspicion.

YANG PIAO: Yes. Someone quickly send for Ts'ai Yung.

SOLDIER: Ts'ai Yung, you're being called for.

Enter TS'AI YUNG.

TS'AI YUNG: I am coming. Field Marshal Yang has sent for me. I must go at once. [*The* SOLDIER *announces him.*] You sent for me, Ministers. What is the matter?

YANG PIAO: Today we have received a secret decree from the Emperor especially requesting you to invite and accompany Tung Cho to the palace to mount the throne. If you succeed in bringing him past the palace gate for us to lay hands on him you will have performed a great service.

TS'AI YUNG: Rest assured. Your humble servant shall rely on his three inches of infallible tongue for persuading Tung Cho to come to the palace. Nothing will prevent it, depend on it. Provided you two are careful also, we'll see this great deed accomplished together.

WANG YÜN: We couldn't be more gratified, Ts'ai Yung. If you're willing to take care of Tung Cho, we will report to His Majesty at once and have a royal decree issued. This must be done without delay.

Exeunt WANG YÜN *and* YANG PIAO.

TS'AI YUNG [*walks about*]: I've just walked along the main street and turned into this side road. Here is the gate of the prime minister's residence. I'll call someone to the door. Is there anybody there?

Enter TUNG CHO *followed by* LI JU *and* ATTENDANTS.

TUNG CHO: Who's that calling at the gate, Li Ju?

LI JU [*listens*]: It's Ts'ai Yung.

TUNG CHO: Ts'ai Yung? Open the side gate, Li Ju, and ask him to come in.

LI JU [*opens the gate*]: Please come inside, Ts'ai Yung.

TUNG CHO: What is it this time, Ts'ai Yung?

TS'AI YUNG [*falls down at his feet*]: I have the honour to report to the Prime Minister that today is an auspicious day. At the Gate of the Silver Terrace the whole court of officials is assembled and respectfully requests that the Prime Minister will come to the palace and ascend the throne.

TUNG CHO [*smiles*]: Good, good, good! So I too am to have my day. Send someone to bring me my official robes.

LI JU [*looks at the robes*]: You must not go to the palace today. These robes have been torn to shreds by worms and mice. If you go to the palace it is bound to spell disaster for you.

TUNG CHO: Ts'ai Yung, I'll not be going to the palace. My official robes have been torn to shreds by worms and mice. I'm afraid they're not fit to wear.

TS'AI YUNG: Prime Minister, this is a sign to cast off the old and change to the new – to change these robes for the dragon robes of an emperor.

TUNG CHO: Ts'ai Yung, you are a man after my own heart. What you've said is true. When I enter the Gate of the Silver Terrace I shall be changing into dragon robes. What need shall I have for these old robes of mine? What Ts'ai Yung says is right; what Li Ju said was wrong. Send someone to open the main gate.

LI JU [*looks at the gate*]: Prime Minister, you must not go out of the house today. The gate is covered all over with spiders' webs inside and out. If you go now, I'm afraid you'll be caught in a web of calamities just like this.

TUNG CHO: Ts'ai Yung, I'll not be coming. There must be some mischief in all this. That's why I saw this bad omen.

TS'AI YUNG: Prime Minister, this is another sign to cast off the old and change to the new. When you come to the Gate of the Silver Terrace and mount the precious throne it'll be you who'll cover the whole kingdom with your web. You'll have no more need for this residence of yours.

TUNG CHO: What Ts'ai Yung says is right; what Li Ju said was wrong. Send someone to bring me my carriage.

LI JU [*looks at the carriage*]: Ah, how is it that this carriage has lost one of its wheels? This means some great misfortune. Prime Minister, you must not ride in your carriage today, or the journey you go on will have no return.

TS'AI YUNG: When you reach the Gate of the Silver Terrace, Prime Minister, with all the hundreds of officials welcoming you you'll change into a carriage drawn by a team of five pairs of horses. This too is a sign meaning to cast off the old and change to the new.

TUNG CHO: What Ts'ai Yung says is right; what Li Ju said was wrong. And if you dare say another word, Li Ju, I'll have your head off!

LI JU: Very well, very well, very well! I've tried in a hundred ways to stop you and you won't listen. This time when you go you'll be bringing death and disaster on yourself and all your clan. And when the time comes don't say Li Ju didn't warn you. [*sighs*] If you are to fail what use is this life to me? This day I take my leave of you, Prime Minister. It is better to dash my head against this carriage and die than fall into the hands of those traitors. [*dashes himself against the carriage and dies*] *Exit.*

ATTENDANT: Your Excellency, Li Ju has dashed his head against the carriage and died.

TUNG CHO: Alas! Li Ju has dashed his head against the carriage and died. Li Ju, my child, you were never destined to enjoy happiness. [*walks about*] Here we are outside the palace gate, Ts'ai Yung. I don't see any hundreds of officials here to welcome me. How is that?

TS'AI YUNG: All the civil and military officials are inside the Gate of the Silver Terrace waiting to receive you there.

TUNG CHO: In that case I shall get down from my carriage and let us proceed through the Gate of the Silver Terrace.

TS'AI YUNG: I shall go ahead and announce you, and bring all the officials high and low out to welcome you.

TUNG CHO: Quite right, quite right!

TS'AI YUNG: Now I'm through the gate. Someone shut the gate! *Exit.*

TUNG CHO: Why did they close the gate when Ts'ai Yung went in? Something must be amiss. I'd better not stay here.

Enter WANG YÜN, YANG PIAO *and* TS'AI YUNG, *followed by* SOLDIERS.

WANG YÜN: Tung Cho, you traitor, where are you going? You know your crimes?

TUNG CHO: What crimes, Wang Yün?

WANG YÜN: Ts'ai Yung, read out the royal decree. Listen, you traitor!

TS'AI YUNG: The Emperor decrees: Being wanting in virtue we the humble descendant of the Great Kingdom have often feared that we might fall on evil times. Years ago General Ho Chin, wishing to deprive the eunuchs of their power, foolishly chose to summon you, a treacherous military commander. You brought soldiers into the palace and abused your power. We have regretted this much to our cost. Fortunately with the help of the spirits of our ancestors Heaven is to put an end to your evil deeds. You will be executed and your body burnt at the crossroads as a warning to all both at home and abroad.

TUNG CHO: It's all up. I must run for my life.

Enter LI SU *with* SOLDIERS.

LI SU: You evil scoundrel, where are you going? Take this! [*drives his spear into* TUNG CHO]

TUNG CHO: Wretched Li Su, wretched Li Su! How dare you take your spear to me? Where's my son Lü Pu?

LÜ PU *rushes in.*

LÜ PU: You villain! Stay where you are! Take this from me! [*drives his spear into him;* TUNG CHO *falls*]

TUNG CHO: I spit on you! What a misfortune to have two such dutiful sons! Why don't you ask my wife Tiao Ch'an to bring a rope to tie me up?

LI SU *and* LÜ PU *tie up* TUNG CHO.

YANG PIAO: Today we have taken Tung Cho and brought peace and power back to the House of Han. Above all we owe this to the marvellous stratagem of Minister Wang.

MUSICAL INSTRUMENTS USED IN YÜAN DRAMA

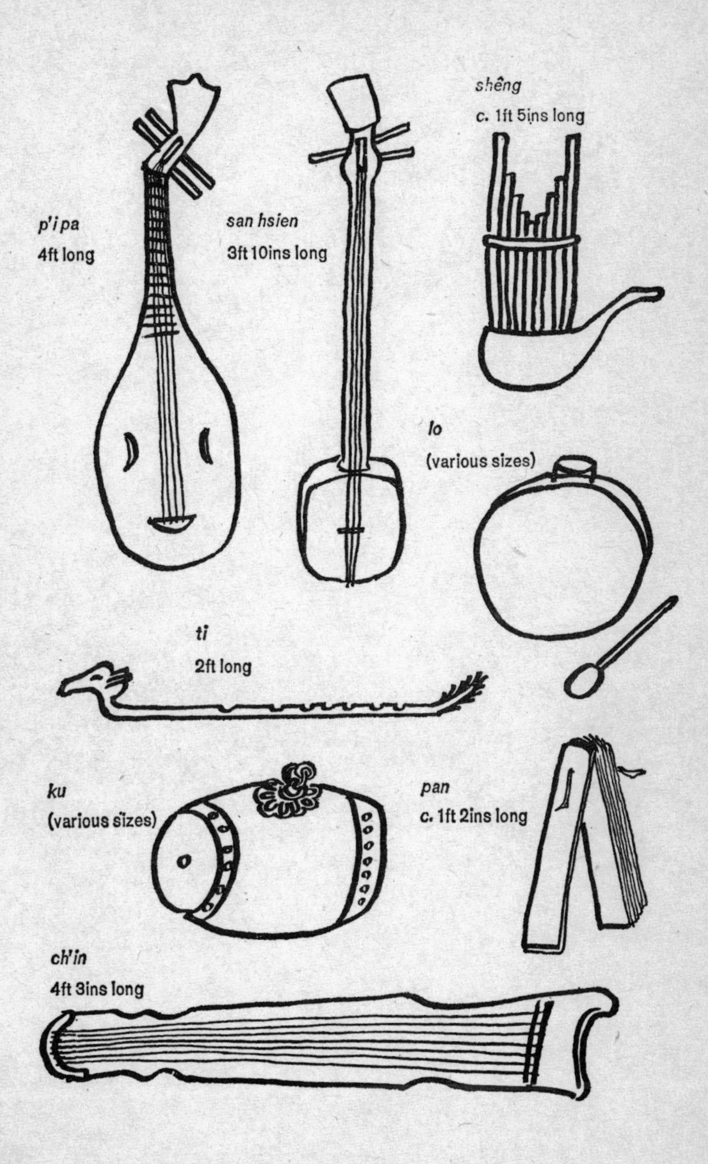

NOTES

THE SOUL OF CH'IEN-NÜ LEAVES HER BODY

1. *Willow-Breaking Pavilion:* The custom was to break off a willow branch and give it to the one who was leaving. The practice probably dates from the third century B.C.
2. *the tortoise-shell divination:* The forecast was 'read' from the cracks that appeared on the carapace when it was heated.

THE INJUSTICE DONE TO TOU NGO

1. *The attendants shout:* It was the practice in Chinese courts for attendants at this point to holloa and shout in order to lend awe to the proceedings.
2. *paper money:* Especially made for the dead.
3. *a white hearse:* White is the colour of mourning in China.
4. *the Three Duties and the Four Virtues:* Being for a woman to obey her father when at home, her husband when she married, and her son when her husband died; to wait on her parents-in-law, respect her husband and master, to live in harmony with her sisters-in-law and at peace with her neighbours.
5. *I shall have you arrested:* Totally incorruptible officials had the power to judge not only the quick but the dead.
6. *courts face the South:* Among other things the South symbolizes justice and magnanimity.

CHANG BOILS THE SEA

1. *iron horses:* Pendants in the shape of horses hung under the eaves.
2. *ch'ing:* A large bowl made either of stone or of bronze.

3. *kuei:* The *Osmanthus fragrans.*
4. *How much more their power over me than the poems of P'an-pan over Huang T'ing-chien:* P'an-pan, a *kuan chi* (a courtesan and a Japanese geisha rolled into one, provided by the government to entertain officials and their guests) of the Sung dynasty, and Huang T'ing-chien (1045–1105), a major poet, wrote a series of *tz'ŭ* poems in reply to each other.
5. *Hsü Fei-chiung:* An immortal maid in ancient mythology famous for her beauty.
6. *twin phoenixes:* Literally a *fêng* and a *lüan.* Of the three hundred and sixty 'feathered creatures' *fêng* stands at the top and *lüan* in the second place – an excellent match.

AUTUMN IN HAN PALACE

1. *Like Herdboy on the Starry Shore awaiting the Spinning Maid's raft:* The constellations of the Herdboy and the Spinning Maid symbolize long separated lovers parted by the Milky Way.
2. *Chang-an:* The capital city.
3. *two farewells:* When someone went on a long journey it was customary for his relatives and friends to select an auspicious day on which they would see him off in a boat that sailed for some distance from the shore and then returned. This was called the first farewell. The date of his actual departure when they saw the traveller off finally was the second farewell.
4. *General Su Wu:* Su Wu (?–60 B.C.) was sent as an emissary to certain Turki tribes and was kept a prisoner for nineteen years.
5. *T'ien Hêng:* An emperor of the Small Kingdom in the second century B.C. who was unwilling to surrender himself to the first Emperor of Han and committed suicide.
6. *the midnight songs of Ch'u:* After joining forces and having conquered the Kingdom of Ch'in in 206 B.C., the leaders of the insurrection, Hsiang Yü of Ch'u and Liu Pang of Han, fought against each other for supremacy. One night when Hsiang Yü and his

troops were besieged they heard the songs of Ch'u being sung in the enemy camp, and finally realized that the land of Ch'u was now completely in the hands of Liu Pang.

A STRATAGEM OF INTERLOCKING RINGS

1. TIAO CH'AN [*bows*]: The gesture consisting of clasping one hand over the other at the right side and then moving them up and down several times. This was the customary greeting for women.

READ MORE IN PENGUIN

In every corner of the world, on every subject under the sun, Penguin represents quality and variety – the very best in publishing today.

For complete information about books available from Penguin – including Puffins, Penguin Classics and Arkana – and how to order them, write to us at the appropriate address below. Please note that for copyright reasons the selection of books varies from country to country.

In the United Kingdom: Please write to *Dept. EP, Penguin Books Ltd, Bath Road, Harmondsworth, West Drayton, Middlesex UB7 ODA*

In the United States: Please write to *Consumer Sales, Penguin USA, P.O. Box 999, Dept. 17109, Bergenfield, New Jersey 07621-0120.* VISA and MasterCard holders call 1-800-253-6476 to order Penguin titles

In Canada: Please write to *Penguin Books Canada Ltd, 10 Alcorn Avenue, Suite 300, Toronto, Ontario M4V 3B2*

In Australia: Please write to *Penguin Books Australia Ltd, P.O. Box 257, Ringwood, Victoria 3134*

In New Zealand: Please write to *Penguin Books (NZ) Ltd, Private Bag 102902, North Shore Mail Centre, Auckland 10*

In India: Please write to *Penguin Books India Pvt Ltd, 706 Eros Apartments, 56 Nehru Place, New Delhi 110 019*

In the Netherlands: Please write to *Penguin Books Netherlands bv, Postbus 3507, NL-1001 AH Amsterdam*

In Germany: Please write to *Penguin Books Deutschland GmbH, Metzlerstrasse 26, 60594 Frankfurt am Main*

In Spain: Please write to *Penguin Books S. A., Bravo Murillo 19, 1° B, 28015 Madrid*

In Italy: Please write to *Penguin Italia s.r.l., Via Felice Casati 20, I–20124 Milano*

In France: Please write to *Penguin France S. A., 17 rue Lejeune, F–31000 Toulouse*

In Japan: Please write to *Penguin Books Japan, Ishikiribashi Building, 2–5–4, Suido, Bunkyo-ku, Tokyo 112*

In Greece: Please write to *Penguin Hellas Ltd, Dimocritou 3, GR–106 71 Athens*

In South Africa: Please write to *Longman Penguin Southern Africa (Pty) Ltd, Private Bag X08, Bertsham 2013*